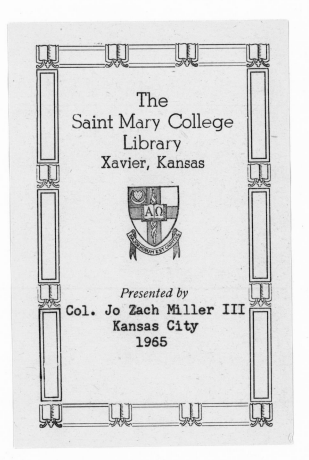

CONCILIUM

THEOLOGY IN THE AGE OF RENEWAL

CONCILIUM

CONCILIUM/VOL. 6

FUNDAMENTAL THEOLOGY

THE
CHURCH
AND THE
WORLD

Volume 6

CONCILIUM
theology in the age of renewal

PAULIST PRESS
NEW YORK, N.Y. / GLEN ROCK, N.J.

CONTENTS

vii

PART II

BIBLIOGRAPHICAL SURVEY

PART III

DO-C: DOCUMENTATION CONCILIUM

PART IV

CHRONICLE OF THE LIVING CHURCH

PREFACE

Johannes B. Metz/*Münster, W. Germany*

Vatican Council II has brought into the limelight the constantly "exposed flank" of the Church and of her theology in its commitment to the world. This section, concerned with those borderline questions on the frontiers of theology, will deal with the very foundations of a deeper understanding and of a more effective proclamation of our faith in its *confrontation* with contemporary philosophical and theological problems. These problems stem from the growing philosophical, social and religious pluralism and the increasing secularization of our world. In this confrontation, theology should serve the hope of contemporary man not only by giving answers, but also by listening and learning, and even often perhaps by re-learning. We assume in this section that today's challenge to theology stems from the very roots of the Christian's understanding of his faith, so that these borderline questions on the frontiers of theology constantly turn into basic and fundamental ones. As such, these questions fall into the scope of Fundamental Theology by its engagement in an unceasing dialogue with the world of our time.

This section therefore represents the discipline of Fundamental Theology, which perhaps more than any other is seeking a new understanding of itself and of its genuine theological character so that it can be faithful to its responsibility for Christian hope (Cf. 1 Pet. 3, 15). In this connection those questions will be

1

treated that are particularly urgent for our time and fall within the scope of this Fundamental Theology, *e.g.,* the possibility, meaning and properties of the act of faith today, both in its interpretation and foundation; the theological analysis of the experience of faith and its interpersonal dimensions; the hermeneutical foundations of theology; the development and historicity of the faith, of the Church and of Christianity; the theological problems concerning the non-Christian religions; and especially those questions concerning atheism and the theological explanation of unbelief and of the present-day ideologies.

The theme of Schema XIII of Vatican Council II, *The Church in the Modern World,* is in a certain sense *the* theme of our section. The contributions to this volume are especially dedicated to those problems that have a broad—or narrow—connection with the theological background of this conciliar theme. (Cf. the essays of Philips, Balthasar, Rahner, Metz and the bibliographical survey of Schlette. The contributions of Bouillard and Nédoncelle are, on the other hand, dedicated to two basic questions of Fundamental Theology.)

PART I

ARTICLES

Gérard Philips / *Louvain, Belgium*

The Church
in the Modern World

One of the most startling proposals made during the debates of Vatican Council II was certainly the suggestion of Cardinal Suenens, presented toward the end of the first session, that we should delineate the Church not only as to its internal structure, but also in its relation to the world. The cardinal in his speech made use of the expressions: *Ecclesia ad intra* and *Ecclesia ad extra,* a manner of speaking that proved to be more approximate than rigorously exact. The proposal aroused real enthusiasm, which was heightened by the pastoral concern of the conciliar Fathers and by the realistic, positive and universalist views of most responsible people in the Church today. As they see it, the Church is not only a fixed entity but a task to be fulfilled. The outside world is keenly interested. No doubt the hopes that have been raised are exaggerated; consequently many prudent people are warning us of probable disappointments.

I

A DIFFICULT PROBLEM

Meanwhile the complexity of the problems to be discussed is more and more evident. Two attempts at composing Schema XIII (formerly XVII) were set aside and, if the third was finally accepted as a basis for discussion, the criticisms were numerous and conflicting, not only as to details but as to substance as well. This is not astonishing. Hitherto, theologians have not given close attention to these complicated questions. Only a few years ago the subject did not seem urgent, so when thinkers were abruptly confronted with it, they were unprepared and more or less divided in opinion with respect to the proposed solutions as well as to the manner of looking at and studying the problem. They were not clearly distinguishing the different levels involved in their objectives: the sacred and the profane, the natural and the supernatural, the Church and the world.

The more difficulties that pile up, the more urgent becomes the need for facing them squarely. Christians are in acute need and are suffering pangs of conscience; whereas the world, more aware than ever before of the fact of the Church, has expectations that cannot be denied. Today the accelerated tempo of new ideas and their rapid communication on a world scale allow for no dilatory tactics. The Church and the Council cannot escape; they must run the risk of an incomplete statement that is sufficiently clear; they must draw up guidelines based on the unchanging but dynamic principles of revelation. In this case the prime concern is not the evangelization of all men. This task was described brilliantly in the Constitution on the Church. Still less is it a question today of an attempt to modernize a Church without regard for its otherworldly vocation; nor is it a covert attempt to win favor with non-believers. The program contains at its very center, beyond any doubt, the *total application of the Gospel message to the earthly life of men,* without losing sight of a destiny that goes beyond this world. How truly apostolic is the involvement of Christians in the world and for the world? And what does this involve by way of the service that Christians must render to society as a whole?

Let us hope that the aim of the Schema is clearly understood and accepted by the majority of the Fathers and theologians at the Council. There will be a few who fear the distraction of earthly preoccupations because they are focusing on the primordial finality of the kingdom of God; while others, who are champions of the humanization of the world, fear that the call of heavenly things may prevent them from exercising fully their role as men. Some have not yet been able to extricate themselves from the mentality of a regime where Church and State are closely united. For these people Schema XIII is hopelessly defective; according to them it goes beyond the ecclesial activity, for which the world is only a means leading to a spiritual perfection that has nothing to do with material things. But these constitute only a small number, mostly from circles that are not open-minded about present-day problems.

Yet, it is extremely important that an agreement be reached at the outset on the meaning of the terms used. Often one has the impression that two parties are confronting each other: the Church on the one side and the world on the other. But when one looks more closely, the two terms are interpenetrating, and besides, the term "world" in Christian language has many different meanings that must be analyzed carefully.

II

STATING THE CASE

1. What Is Meant by the Church?

Presumably the readers of conciliar decrees do not all see the same reality in the Church. First of all, believing Catholics view it literally as the continuation of Christ's saving mystery, at the same time recognizing in it a visible organization, the ecclesial Roman community. Others, to whom the Council also speaks, see in the Church not an object of faith, but a vast social and human influence of a group of religious men. They are concerned either with recognizing its services or loosening its grip on the masses. As the Council addresses first one part of its audience and then another, it changes its attitudes, and it is important to be fully aware of this.

The first object of the Schema is to lead the faithful to enter wholeheartedly the human and temporal tasks of society. Beyond

that, however, is glimpsed a much wider audience of non-Catho-
lics, non-Christians and non-believers with whom the Church
would like to enter into dialogue. In common with them there is
work to be done for the welfare of all men on earth. Schema XIII
aims at outlining the reasons for this work, and does not concern
the why and the how of the work of evangelization, which is written into the very nature of the Church and which it will never
deny or neglect. It proposes further to apply to "intra-mundane"
life the lights and principles drawn from Christ's message, with
the explicit intention of better understanding and improving the
human condition by collaboration that is sincere and effective
with all men.

Even on this level, the Church has something to say to the
world, and the world does not always refuse to listen. Of course
the Church must seek first the kingdom of God, but it knows that,
if it is faithful, all the rest will be added unto it. What is more, it
is legitimately convinced that it could not perform its primary
mission, if it did not rouse in its members, on behalf of all their
human brethren, a spirit of disinterested mutual help. Even for
the non-believer, even for the atheist or one who thinks himself
such, the Church is a spiritual force with which it may be useful
to cooperate, and in any case one would be foolish to scorn its
contribution to the gradual solution of human problems. We can
mention the safeguarding of the dignity of the human person, social and cultural progress, the protection of the family, the
strengthening of world peace. All these interest believers as well
as those who profess no religion. On both sides enlightened
people realize the need of working together, if we do not wish to
perish together.

The Church speaks to the world in the name of God and Christ,
but it does *not* require a profession of faith in its creed before
starting work in areas common to all men. If God in Christian
preaching is a God of justice and charity, the Christian Church
cannot be indifferent when confronted with human misery. The
Samaritan of the parable does not ask the wounded man picked
up by the wayside for a declaration of orthodoxy: he comforts

him, cares for him and tries to heal him without ulterior or self-centered motives.

Even so it would be wrong to ask the Church to disguise meanwhile its true identity and to hide from the world the source of its inspiration and devotedness. It need not be ashamed of Christ whose name it bears and whose doctrine it spreads. Its foundation in faith dedicates it to the service of God and not primarily to the service of men, but it assures them the greatest of benefits by bestowing on them divine life—charity, which transforms their earthly existence. It does not preach the worship of humanity, but an authentic humanism will be the fruit of its preaching.

To proclaim this program, the Council need not be embarrassed or reticent. It has no intention of replacing the United Nations, when it speaks to all men and all nations in the name of Christ in order to promote the good of all. It has no secret desire to exercise power, but rather a sincere wish to be of service.

2. *What Is Meant by the World?*

In the language of Scripture, and consequently in the language of Christians and especially preachers, the term "world" may be used in an unfavorable sense, without losing sight of the original term meaning the *totality of God's creative work*. Now creation is good: the biblical teaching is far from any taint of Manichaeism. It is only that in the course of history the men who people God's world have fallen into sin. This has spread to such a degree as to become an evil power, opposed to God by its intellectual and moral attitudes, without however removing it from the sovereign domain of the creator. The world under the sign of the evil one is inimical to God and bad by definition. If the world listened to the Word and rejected its sin, it would no longer be the "world". Hence, in the authors of the New Testament, especially in St. John, there are dualistic tendencies not ontologically speaking, but in the moral and spiritual order, which might mislead readers not used to Johannine style and its symbolism. St. John asserts in the same breath that we must detest the world and its wiles, and that God so loved the world as to give his only Son in order to save it. The two uses of the same term, however conflicting they may appear, are harmonized in salvation history. The world, created good by God, became bad because of the misuse of human freedom, without losing hope of recovery. For the merciful love of God is stronger than sin. It is above all to the evil world that the Son of God incarnate addressed his message of salvation. Accepted in faith, this message saves the world and re-establishes it in friendship with the Father.

The Bible teaches us that we should hate the *wicked* world, precisely because we must love the world that came from the hand of God and bring it back to its author. We not only are to recover its original goodness, but raise it to a level that is much higher by means of the grace of redemption.

There is, moreover, a second distinction that one cannot neglect without causing grave misunderstanding. The "world" means also the *totality of all men* living on the earth. Among them are saints and rascals. Christians are a part of this world that they cannot get away from, even while opposing the evil principles that all too often direct the lives of men. The Christian's separation from the world is in the spiritual order, not the sociological. The Church, likewise, without being part of the evil world because of its heavenly origin, is distinct from the world of sin but not from the men who are sinners, since it is for them that it exists. It cannot be said that it is *confronting* the world: it is established in the midst of the world and the faithful are intermingled with all men. The title of Schema XIII avoids deliberately the expression: the Church *confronting* the world; it speaks of the Church *in* the world today. By its deepest impulsion, the Church tends toward drawing the world back to its original unity, until it is identified with it, until that time comes when the plan for its restoration is wholly accomplished, when the redeemed universe is given back by the Son to his Father. To claim that the Church is alien to the world of men is to reduce it to an abstract phantom and consequently to destroy it.

By the "world" is understood *all earthly values and those tasks* that men must accomplish in the temporal order. These values are not static; they involve, on man's part, the duty of developing them in the direction willed by their author; they are the continuation of the creative work by human effort. These values and this work are not vitiated in themselves. This realm has its own importance and value, though it is certainly temporary and not ultimate. We are then faced with a genuine autonomy of the temporal, not an absolute autonomy but a real one nevertheless. The realm of earthly values has its own principles and is ruled by interior laws that are worthy of respect, which no pretext of piety can reduce to a mere means of promoting religion. This principle is basic to the distinction of the two societies: the Church and the human community. This distinction offers no reason for hostile separateness. If human society sets itself up as an absolute power, it means totalitarianism and the pagan cult of the powerful.

But on the other hand, to speak of the relations between the Church and the world does not mean, for the Christian, trying to harmonize his profession of faith with his profane existence, as if it concerned two mutually exclusive compartments. It is in the world that a life proves itself Christian. In order to participate in the life of the world, the baptized person does not have to leave the Church. On the contrary, it is precisely at this moment that his belonging to a Church and a religion will show itself. Otherwise charity would remain sterile.

The Church lives in the world and with the world. It will not present itself as a mere bearer of ethereal curiosities. It will have to be involved in the world, not the world of sin, but the one created by God, disfigured by sin, redeemed by Christ. It is responsible for spreading throughout the universe the restoration effected by the Savior. It does not set itself up between the world and God, but attaches the world to God. Likewise, the laity are not the bridge between the Church and the world, but make the Church present in the world. This movement toward unity is not finished: it has just begun. But in the end the redeemed world and the Church will be one.

3. *The Modern World*

In any historical period the Church lives in the world that is its "contemporary". Hence, it is not facing today a problem that is unprecedented. But as the world changes, in turn the problem changes appearance. We find ourselves facing the consequences of the Church's historicity. The awareness of this has become, thank God, more lively among Catholics. They are engaged more than ever in reading the signs of the times. But to prevent any misunderstanding, they must realize that they look at the present world with Christian eyes. Their analysis of facts is guided by the light of faith. This attitude of mind is legitimate, and far from preventing them from being perfectly objective, it requires it. The description of the same human miseries leads a Marxist to a totally anti-Christian attitude, and a Christian to a more generous involvement inspired by his religious convictions. Where the Marxist finds only disastrous alienation, the Christian discovers stepping-stones for proclaiming Christ.

In fact, since the end of World War II we have with us *a new man,* profoundly affected by the latest scientific and technical advances. As a result of the discovery of atomic energy and the conquest of space, he has not simply acquired a new way of feeling, thinking and living: he has literally become someone else and he scarcely recognizes himself. It would be wrong to generalize too much. Really there exist *several worlds* today that are profoundly differentiated, above all, that of the well-off and that of the starving. Too often we are inclined to give in to Europeanism, in spite of our declared intercontinental solidarity and in spite of our goodwill. Thinking on a world scale is a fine program, rarely lived up to in fact. We are slow in recognizing in mission lands the new Churches called, like us, to perfect catholicity. Above all, we are disconcerted and disarmed, as it were, by the people of the Third-World whom we cannot understand. We want to help them and for the most part we succeed only in exasperating them. It is all too easy to complain of the lack of gratitude from our protégés. That is precisely the error: wanting to act as protectors. It is not enough to furnish Asia and Africa with consumer goods, nor even machines and experts. They must be assured of being able to create for themselves a fully human life. From the outset we must give them that higher life of the spirit without which no man can live.

This higher gift presupposes spiritual, moral and religious endowments capable of being enriched and purified. People described as primitive, possess treasures of wisdom, the heritage of preceding generations. Why destroy them instead of bringing them up to a level of development that is more genuine and more universal?

The fact is, however, that modern man in certain classes of society and more or less on all continents has come to be a man without God. He has no more need of God and often considers him an enemy. An *atheism* does exist, one that is not only lived but preached, organized and militant. This is a fact that has never before been recorded in history. Yet, we must look at it very carefully in order to ascertain its true character.

It is very rare for people to get along without an absolute to which they relate. That is why we have an array of new substitute religions being set up nearly everywhere. The cult of duty, collectivity, heroism without reward, the social welfare of the generations to come—these values, considered mandatory, take the place of a God who is impossible to recognize in the usual images that represent him almost as an idol; some treat him as a general repairman who makes up for what is lacking in human activity. Such a divinity does not rise above the order of cosmic phenomena.

The philosopher-theologian Tillich called this conception (of God) supranaturalism, a pure construction of the imagination. Bultmann made popular the idea of demythologizing, and reduced religion to a projection of existential experiences. Bonhoeffer called an end to all "religion", as the product of wishful thinking, when he preached a Christianity without worship. In none of these descriptions can one find the mysterious essence of the Church. It does not sacrifice to the idols that modern thinkers naïvely try to overturn. All such fantasies are left behind by one who knows the true God and who at least grasps the meaning of salvation and eternal life.

But in order to reach this state the believer must have made some corrections in the representations of the divinity with which childhood teaching made him familiar. As an adult, the images of the little catechism no longer suffice. Unfortunately his religious training has usually not kept up with his intellectual development. He thinks he is an atheist while, without knowing it, he is seeking an absolute that is none other than God! The very fact that he is a man forces him to seek a value that dominates and frees him at the same time.

The world, said to be a-religious, whether it admits it or not, suffers a deep anguish, at least when confronted with death. It is not only the atomic bomb that is frightening: we are waging war with an enigma that we cannot solve: what is the meaning of life? of the world? of man? Where are we all going in the last analysis? Would the only answer be: all is absurd, a source of eternal disillusionment?

The Anglican Bishop Robinson has taken pains to explain that God does not live above the world, somewhere among the celestial spheres, nor even simply beyond the universe where the imagination loses itself in nothingness. He is none other than the very foundation of our existence, our ultimate *raison d'être,* and it is on the horizontal dimension that it behooves us to seek him, in our vocation to become "a man for others", a vocation of which Christ seems to us to be the prototype. The success of the little work *Honest to God* is rich in lessons. Modern man is far from being as indifferent before ultimate problems as a pessimistic view had led us to believe.

But in other respects the exposé of Robinson is disappointing. As a professional exegete he might have referred to the Psalms describing so marvelously the omnipresence of God at the very heart of creation and in the heart of man. And yet God is not enclosed within creation. St. Augustine might have shown the bishop that God is closer to me than I am to myself. For a long while serious Christians have been trying desperately, without ever succeeding wholly, to go beyond the categories of time and space. They know, St. Thomas is there to explain it to them, that transcendence and immanence are intertwined in reality.

To speak as if we sought God in the clouds or in a vacuum, there where the world stops, is to treat us like children. To add that henceforth we shall discover God in a horizontal dimension, as if he were at our feet, is to be lost in a mirage that is almost as foolish. Robinson is not the victim of this illusion. His work offers only a vague exposition, suited to a hurried reader, of the much more profound views of Paul Tillich.

The fact remains that the Anglican prelate succeeded in meeting the minds of today's men and in reviving the religious response that was thought to be lost forever.

If the Church wants to speak to the world, it cannot escape the problem of *atheism,* whether real or imaginary. The Church is neither above nor outside of the world. It is from within the world and within man himself that it directs us toward the discovery of our true selves. The Church is a perpetual gift of divine goodness that founded and supports it. It does not artificially create this fundamental seeking. It awakens in our souls a latent question and in this way it challenges the world. If it does not manage to release in man that primordial drive, all its teaching will be unintelligible and will remain a dead letter. But just when man is made to feel his radical insufficiency, it offers him a way out of his anguish. The Church did not invent this answer nor create it; it received it from the mouth of the Son of God.

4. *The Meeting of Church and World*

Dialogue begins with the *posing of basic questions.* Within each one of the faithful the Church finds the anxious world. The baptized person is not the happy possessor of an evident truth. He, too, awaits and accepts the message as a release from an anguished situation. Were this not the case, he would not feel personally called upon. Often, to be sure, this realization is reached only after a salutary crisis.

The Church wants also to contact non-believers and bring them to listen to the Word. To succeed in this mission, it must do more than adopt their modern idiom, their categories of thought and expression; it must leave the primordial universal state of questioning (problématique) and cross, together with them, the region of intellectual and moral darkness in order to arrive at the light. Even then one must take into account what St. Paul calls the scandal and folly of the cross. The wicked world under the influence of the spirit of darkness will oppose the message and fight against it. No believer will be surprised at this; he knows by personal experience the power of resistance that the Word must overcome even in the mind and heart of one who is sincerely disposed to believe. The foreseen contradiction is not, for the Church, a reason to remain silent. On the contrary the inevitable opposition fortifies it in advance against the temptation of relying on its own means of persuasion, instead of counting on the power of him by whom the Christian is sent.

The Church therefore meets the world of non-believers *in the area of broad human values*. Its mission of charity commands it to be at the service of all in order to assist them in reaching a life truly worthy of being called human. Certainly, it could not without contradicting its essence and its vocation establish itself on a purely natural level. It lives in the realm of grace. This does not prevent it from respecting wholly the values that are proper to human nature. Far from denying or destroying them, it strengthens and ennobles them.

The Church will not hesitate in presenting to all an openly Christian anthropology, in which, however, the non-Christian will recognize the basic characteristics that are dear to him and which he would not want to lose under any circumstances. After this, a dialogue can begin and pave the way for sincere cooperation, respecting the personal conscience of each. To be wildly agitated at the possible mistakes of non-believers betrays a lack of confidence in the power of truth and in the basic honesty of man. Man needs to be enlightened and helped: that is precisely

why the Church speaks to him, not to take the place of his conscience but to guide and strengthen it. It is mostly through its
adult members that the Church reveals the efficacy of its teaching
for preventing and curing any alienation. It helps a man, whoever he may be, to find himself with all his responsibilities, duties
and rights.

The ideal is not to aim at coexistence, the mere juxtaposition
of two foreign bodies, but to will to live together, *Mitsein,* as the
Germans say, which invites real collaboration. The Church brings
to this a means of action exceeding the strength of both the man-
in-the-world and the Church itself. This power it receives from
the Spirit who teaches it to be humble and serviceable at the
school of Christ the Servant. In putting these energies to the service of all, it does not quietly attempt to "sacralize" nor "ecclesify"
the world, but it assures profane realities a transcendant dimension by relating them to their origin and last end. Christians
would be guilty before the world if they left it the task of building
itself and refused their indispensable support.

Let me insist, while speaking of dialogue with others, on the
necessity of organizing similar *colloquia* within the bosom of the
Church, between diverse groups and opposing tendencies. Diver-
gent views can create huge problems but they can also enrich the
common action after reaching an equilibrium. Hierarchy and
laity do not oppose but complete each other. Let us not pass over
in silence the particular concerns of those whom we shall call, for
want of a better name, traditionalists and progressives. They need
each other. If they are separated, it will be disastrous. The former,
anxious to keep intact the deposit of revelation, risk not making
use of the treasures at hand and becoming atrophied in immo-
bility. The latter, because they are pursuing new ideas and adapt-
ing to new situations, risk losing the essential and sacrificing to
relativism at the expense of intellectual continuity and truth itself.
Life does not begin again with each new generation, starting from
pure nothingness, neither in the life of the body nor in that of the
mind, nor especially in that of society. Those who insist so much

on the historicity of the Church would do well to think of this. History creates the new, it is true, but this is done by handing on the life of the past to the present and the future.

III

THE CONTENT OF MESSAGE-DIALOGUE

The Church, in speaking to the world that it invites to dialogue, puts in the foreground the *vocation of man,* understanding this in its deepest sense; otherwise the dignity of the person would have no solid guarantee. The human person, who holds the center of general interest today, cannot be fulfilled except in the midst of society. If he closes in on himself, he will perish in narcissism or sterile solipsism. All men are created in the image of the first-born and are called to resemble him ever more and more in their personal engagement and collective effort. Work is their nobility and their title to glory, provided that in working they do not obstruct the opening toward higher regions, nor those where our brothers dwell. If they do not wish to become the slaves of their technical success, let them not close their eyes to those real, culpable defects that the Church calls sin, egoism, and covetousness, which impede the progress of humanity.

The Christian will be the first to become fully a *man among men.* But no one has the right to force him, in order to succeed, to lose sight of his divine vocation and to give up prayer. The least endowed of mortal men is still capable of responding to the call to live as a son of God and at the same time a brother to all. For a Christian must continually promote harmony between his earthly tasks and his destiny beyond the earth, and this must be evident in his actions. The world will scarcely hold it against Christianity for aiming too high, but it might, not without reason, accuse many Christians of not taking their Christian life in the world with enough seriousness.

The Church is at the service of God. Because of this, and not in spite of its religious mission, it is at the service of men. The

God whom it adores is the source of a charity that penetrates the
believer in order to transform him, that brings men back to the
Father by an enveloping movement of unifying love. The Gospel
commands the Church to insist on equality and liberty for all.
It does not hesitate to assert that the organization of temporal
society is not its responsibility. The power of God over the earthly
domain is boundless; that of the Church is not. Moreover it makes
no claim to this: there is no cause for anxiety in this regard. In
our day any ecclesiastical imperialism is doomed to failure. The
modern situation spares the Church any temptation of this kind.

The *humanization of the world* is not an obstacle for the
Church, but an advantage. Inversely, Christianity will help men
to reach a higher level of humanity without taking away from
anyone his personal responsibility. The Church wants adults, not
children to be protected.

The Christian is convinced that *morality* cannot in the last analysis get along without a solid foundation and essential norms;
without these it will dissolve in subjectivism. He knows, too, that
true charity begins with an unlimited respect for justice, and far
from avoiding contacts with his fellowmen, he asks for nothing
more than to work in concert with them.

His conscience has become more sensitive to faults of omission
and appreciates more than ever poverty of spirit. Evangelical
poverty in no wise extols pauperism, still less the exploitation of
extreme want. A subhuman poverty exists which the Gospel tells
every man to relieve with all his might, even to the point of detachment and unmeasured generosity.

The Church does not fear to soil its hands by touching the most
miserable people in order to lift them up. It refuses partnership
with no partner (either individual or group) that brings to dialogue sincerity of heart. The period of the ghetto, when an atmosphere of siege reigned, is henceforth a thing of the past.

It is not enough to proclaim in a solemn charter the rights of
man without distinction of race, sex or social rank. Nowadays,
the *situation of the laborers,* at least in countries that are indus-
trialized, has been considerably improved. Yet this state of uplift

is far from reaching all parts of the globe, and respect for the person of the worker is still an idyllic dream for many. As long as he is obliged, in order to live, to sell his work like merchandise, and as long as he is not treated as an associate in the enterprises and in the building up of society, the objective has not been reached, and the condition of countless masses is well below human, comparable in fact to slavery.

Man cannot improve or develop except in a *family* where conjugal love and fecundity bravely accepted turn the home into a true sanctuary. For the Christian, marriage is a share in the mystery of the love of Christ and the Church. In this domain problems and anguish of conscience are particularly acute. Spouses and parents have the right to expect from the Church, not only words of comfort, but also unequivocal directives on the principles governing family life. Such an answer, clear though it may be, will not excuse a man or woman from the indispensable need to reach a personal decision after careful reflection in the sight of God. Easy solutions would be deceiving, and mere casuistry would only deaden their consciences. The whole problem must be subjected to a respectful examination. All elements should be taken into consideration and all aspects of a particular act considered in the whole context of the individual life. No expert in theology, philosophy, biology or sociology is justified in escaping the common search for solutions. The population explosion has taken on disconcerting proportions. As an answer to this, one cannot rely only on trust in divine providence; it is pure Pharisaism if one does not exert oneself to create new means of subsistence. It would be an even greater crime if one urged young people to organize a kind of national suicide by suppressing life in embryo. Modern technical skill is capable, if it tries, of furnishing the hungry with nourishment, but the sacrifices urgently required will be enormous for all. Meanwhile, let us be careful not to stifle the generosity of those whom we call the great heroes of modern times, namely, the fathers and mothers of families. It is terribly sad to see parents of large families exposed to ridicule; they suffer sometimes from a mild scorn on the part of brethren who think themselves to be Christians. Moreover it is disquieting to see theologians who call themselves Catholics openly expressing doubts about the indissolubility of marriage.

Obviously there is also a hunger that is of the spirit. An intelligent exchange of *cultural goods,* with respect for the great diversity of civilizations, will increase appreciably the productivity of the humanistic heritage. In this realm missionary work has proven to be an incomparably powerful civilizing factor in the course of history. The objective of missionaries, of course, is none other than the spreading of the Christian message that grants to all men the nobility of divine sonship by adoption. This fact must be applied to the building up of profane society where true fraternity must reign.

With regard to society, the encyclicals *Mater et Magistra* and *Pacem in Terris* have put the official seal on such key words of our time as: socialization, humanization, universalism. They echo the doctrine of the Mystical Body, the incarnation and the universal precept of charity, at those points where these salvific events touch earthly history. Otherwise the Word of God on our lips and by our fault would become a falsehood. On this point the Council will have to speak to the world with complete frankness, and with virile courage, if it wishes to prevent, in the case of numberless readers, a baneful disappointment.

When the Church proclaims that the very Son of God became a man among men, exactly like all others except for sin, it emphasizes the *solidarity* of the human race in all its extension. Consequently, rich nations must share their goods with needy peoples, without humiliating them and without reducing them to a gilded servitude. The emergency plans drawn up by the international community brook no delay in their application. The peace of the world, always precarious, is at stake. The reliance on nuclear arms, for the so-called general security, amounts to a gesture of despair that might annihilate humanity. The balance of power by fear is very dangerous. And yet it will not do to plunge into an illusory pacifism, well-meaning perhaps, but marred by a woeful lack of realism. The task of the Council will be hard, and the work of bringing peace to men's minds is the first duty that presents itself.

Under the influence of ecclesial renewal and conciliar work, Catholics are beginning to understand better their vocation in the world and for the world. By neglecting their earthly tasks they disfigure the creative order established by God and restored by Christ. At the same time, Catholics are learning to make a clearer distinction between their strictly ecclesial mission and the mature program of action that they have to realize now in the world. An adult Christianity no longer has recourse to ecclesiastical triumphalism. In the light of the Gospels it grasps more clearly the meaning of New Testament themes such as witness (*martyria*), service (*diakonia*) and communion (*koinonia*)—and, please God, Christians are not mumbling these beautiful Greek words but are making their content pass over into their daily lives.

By putting on the agenda the Schema "The Church in the Modern World," the Council offers proof of a realistic attitude and a pastoral solicitude that does not shirk its responsibilities. But a Council cannot congratulate itself on having succeeded unless the whole community translates into concrete living the teaching proposed, which is drawn directly from the source of mystery, the Son of God incarnate, for the salvation of the whole world.

Hans Urs von Balthasar / *Switzerland*

Meeting God
in Today's World

The Church of today is earnestly striving to encounter the modern world. When two men meet each other, each wishes to experience what the other is and what the other can mean for him. The two know in advance that they are both men, and they bring this knowledge as a presupposition to the meeting. But when Church and world are to meet each other, it is not so easy to obtain anticipatory knowledge of this sort. For the Church is Church only in the world, that is, as a part or aspect of the world; and the world is world (whether it knows it or not) only as "created through and unto him" (Col. 1, 16). Consequently, the two can never be altogether distinguished from one another; neither can they be altogether identical in any respect. The question of what is Church in the Church and what is secular in the world cannot be answered immediately. It can be answered, if at all, only after searching discussion. Was it entirely clear to Augustine, for example, just what was the nature of the *Civitas hujus mundi?*

Today we commonly speak of the "secular world". One must be careful to note that this is not a tautology; neither is it an expression of hostility. The adjective does not conceal a polemical edge that the noun does not have. Still, if the expression is correctly used, the adjective does have a coloration which the noun, at least in its everyday use, does not have. Or if the noun does

23

have this meaning it is submerged, or rightly or wrongly it has become noticeable to men and especially to Christians only in the modern world.

If we inquire into the theological truth of this expression, two general considerations present themselves: (1) It is more difficult for modern man than it was for previous generations to see the world as an epiphany, as a revelation of, and a reference to, God. (2) Christianity played a part in this change.

1. Paul's two main statements about the pagans' knowledge of God (Acts 17, 16-30; Rom. 1, 18-22) require that the knowable (*gnôston*) God be revealed (*phaneron*) by means of a revelatory *act* of God (*theos gar autois ephanerôsen*). The revelation consists in this, that ever since the world began, what is invisible in him is seen through his works, for it *allows* itself to be seen (*kathoratai*). Of course this is visible only to the thinking-seeing understanding of man (*noumena*). Paul's statement deals with ontology, and holds "ever since the world began". In other words, it is grounded in the very nature of this world. Paul's position is developed and clarified in his address at the Areopagus. God dwells in the heaven and the earth, which he has made, and not in temples built by men (Acts 17, 24), so that his reality is "not far from each one of us"; rather "in him we live and move, and have our being", and therefore we are told to "seek" him, and that perhaps we will "touch" something of "the divine" (*to theion:* Acts 17, 29), and in this way will find him (Acts 17, 27). The immanence of God in his creation, which is the basis for our immanence in him, is here also described as a matter of ontology; and therefore it cannot be rendered problematic by the passage of time, nor can it be reduced or annulled in a post-Christian era. This is especially the case since the proximity of God (Acts 17, 27) has manifested itself as a desire for greater closeness with the sending of the man-Jesus. Moreover, it is ordered to a decisive appearance of God on the day when the world is judged according to his justice (Acts 17, 31). Thus, we cannot say that a change has taken place in God's ontological and personal presence in the world—as though we would speak of his absence, or of something

of that sort, a withdrawal of God out of the world and into himself (which would be metaphysically absurd), a cancellation of God's immanence (and thus of God's revelation) in creation. This would have as its consequence the immediate annihilation of creation.

If men claim to find it somehow more difficult or impossible to behold God through his creation, in the Pauline sense, the reason for this cannot be that Paul was speaking in a time-conditioned way to the Greeks or to ancient man in general, to men whose spiritual vision was in this respect specially privileged. Theologically, basic scriptural affirmations (the Psalms and the Book of Wisdom also make such affirmations) are not to be relativized by reference to changing historical conditions. What then did this spiritual vision actually behold?

In the early, "mythical" period, despite all the mystery and terror of suffering and death, being was surrounded with such a luminosity—in its highest moments at least existence was so much a gift and a kindness—that being could not be explained otherwise than by means of the presence of "a God". Subsequently, in the "philosophical" period, there was the overwhelming force of the order of the world, the radiant mathematical harmony shining forth most purely in the stars, untouched by the randomness of matter. Man's small intellect was not then the measure of all things; rather it had to look to a higher, divine intellect, which worked providentially in all things and revealed itself in the order of the world. One may ask: What of all this is supposed to have changed for us? Why is the modern scientist (who surely does not create the laws for which he is searching) not obliged to stand in wonder before a world order that indefinitely transcends his intellect?

If nothing can change in God's ontological relationship to the world and in the basic orientation of the human spirit toward God, whence the complaint that God is becoming less visible, the complaint about the "eclipse of God" in our time? Our initial answer is tentative and preliminary: the source of the complaint is the changed relationship of man to the things of the world.

These no longer inspire him to rise through contemplation to the absolute. Rather, they provide the opportunity for practical mastery through technology. In the first relationship, the human spirit looks *through* things and above; in the second, it looks down *to* things from its transcending height.

Western intellectual history has created a philosophy for both relationships. Nicholas of Cusa has formulated this in the following very concise way. Man's created spirit is an image of God according to the following proportion: as God the creator is to the real created world that he has produced from his essence and his ideas, so the human spirit (as *secundus deus*) is to an unreal world, *i.e.*, to the world of numbers (and thus to the mathematical-physical-technological mastery of the world), which man creates out of the similarly archetypal unity of his spirit. This excellent formula, simultaneously bringing into focus the *grandeur* and the *misère* of man, is a variation of the ancient conception of man as a microcosm. Man is an epitome of the universe, and because of this is the world-transcending "boundary" (*methorion*) between God and the world.

Plotinus, for example, summing up the whole philosophical tradition of antiquity, describes the human spirit as follows: it is drawn above itself in eternal desire (*erôs ephesis*) for the absolute by its intellectual activity. Below, it produces out of itself and recapitulates in itself the entire physical and material multiplicity of the world, not only the numbers but the natural forms as well. (If one simply thinks of this process as evolutionary, one has the system of Soloviev or of Teilhard de Chardin.) Thus the idea that man is the epitome of the world is not at all modern. It is to be found in its entirety in antiquity and in the patristic era (Origen, Augustine, Gregory the Great, Maximus). From these sources it enters the Middle Ages, and was strongly reiterated in the Renaissance and in the Baroque era.

With Kant it received an accidental modification. Now only the downward view is "scientific", the view into a world that has arisen out of the spirit and which has been molded by the spirit in a predominately mathematical and technological way. The view upward is now ethical and existential rather than scientific. The attempt of idealism from Fichte to Hegel to understand the upward view once again in the ancient, theoretical manner came to grief because this idealism postulated an identity between the human and the divine self; and therefore the structure of the view downward (controlling reason—*Verstand*) was universalized, and it determined the structure of the vision upward (receptive understanding—*Vernunft*). God is analyzed in the same way that one analyzes the things of the world. But basically this is already so close to atheism that the transition from Hegel to Feuerbach and Marx is hardly noticeable.

Modern intellectual history is to this extent tragic. The intellectual vision of God in the world (in St. Paul's sense) was first shaken in a significant way by Nominalism, a revolution of theologians against the alleged intrusion of philosophical understanding. Nominalism already denied any philosophically based knowledge of God. To counter this, the intervention of antiquity was sought in ever new ways, from Cusa and Ficino to Goethe, Hölderlin and Heidegger. In classical and romantic art, antiquity's vision of a theophanous world was made to live again. But this metaphysical perception of God through the things of the world is (and always has been) a strain (*ephesis, oreksis*), really a conversion (*epistrophê*) or a "swimming against the stream" (Bergson). It is an action that is repugnant to a mind that habitually and ever more intensively looks down from its own high station. The expression of this repugnance is the theoretical (Kant) and practical dissolution of metaphysics that has gone so far that metaphysics is considered nonexistent, superfluous, and impossible when set along side what are called the exact sciences (*i.e.,* the natural sciences).

How unhealthy this situation is for the human understanding is most clearly evident from what has happened to the humane disciplines (so-named in contrast to the natural sciences), consequent to the death of metaphysics. Without anyone's noticing it, they have practically ceased to exist as they have more and more subjected themselves to the methodology of the natural sciences.

The humane disciplines are the understanding of the self-expression of the free human spirit, to the extent that it is a sovereign microcosm and thus *methorion* ("boundary") to God. This position of the human spirit in the cosmos can be conceived only by metaphysics. If it is denied, man's spirit descends to become a secular *servus servorum*. It puts itself in the service of the things of the world, which are supposed to be serving man. It is therefore evident that there can be no meaningful dialogue between the natural sciences and Christian theology where the mediating role of metaphysics *and* of the autonomous humane disciplines is no longer recognized.

2. We said that Christianity was not without responsibility in this modern development. For man was imbedded in the theophanous world, and Christianity jarred him out of it by placing over against him as a person the living, personal God, who is above the world and who directly reveals himself to man. Christianity places man in a relationship which leaves far behind the services of a metaphysical knowledge of God and makes this practically superfluous. Therefore, theological metaphysics actually died the day Christ was born.

Heidegger asserts that a Christian metaphysics is a contradiction, since one who already knows God can no longer honestly ask about the mystery of being. Karl Barth says the same thing, since the philosophical quest can never lead to the knowledge of the only true, living God. The two are approaching a single state of affairs from opposite sides. The difficulty of this problem is not to be underestimated. The problem is not solved, it is only made more difficult by the fact that Christianity took possession of the God-fearing philosophy of antiquity, in order to perfect and elevate it through revelation, and thereby to set it right. For a long time that may have appeared edifying, but the day had to come—and it did come but a short time after the death of Aquinas—when puzzled men would ask: Whence comes all this certain knowledge which the understanding suddenly has about God?

Modern Christianity concealed the problem from itself by having pre-Christian antiquity once again play its concert with full orchestra, in order to make the congruence between natural and supernatural theology credible. But then the game was over. It had begun on the Areopagus: "For as I was going about and observing objects of your worship, I found also an altar with this inscription: 'To the Unknown God'. What therefore you worship in ignorance, that I proclaim to you" (Acts 17, 23). The Greeks seek as "philosophers" what Paul as a "theologian" knows. His knowledge comes not from the Being of beings, but from Judaeo-Christian history. In the old covenant God has, through his actions, revealed himself as a living subject in contrast to human subjects; in the new covenant a human subject so conducted himself vis-à-vis other human persons that his claim that he was God's Son and God himself appeared credible.

In every major period of its history, Christianity has set the Bible's greater knowledge of God in critical opposition to the metaphysical knowledge about the mystery of being. *Si comprehendis non est Deus*, Augustine warns, as do the Greek Fathers. Gregory the Great speaks in the same vein. So does the tradition of Dionysius the Areopagite, which was renewed again and again during the Latin Middle Ages and came down to Nicholas of Cusa. The great saints' guiding experience of God is evidence that from a Christian point of view this was right: a Benedict, who gave Christian existence the form of humble worship; a Francis, who—on the basis of a Christian experience of God and in opposition to any form of pantheism—perceived and greeted the presence of the God of love through his brother and sister creatures; an Ignatius of Loyola, for whom the contemplation of the Christian mysteries of salvation opened onto the cosmos (in the *Contemplatio ad obtinendum amorem*).

Ignatius experienced the universe as an epiphany, as a gift of the God who gives himself, as the dwelling of the God who is immanent in all things, as produced by the God who "labors" in all things. Almost after the manner of Plotinus, Ignatius experienced the universe as light streaming or water flowing forth from God himself. And how could the theology of the schools or the piety and spirituality of mysticism let itself be hemmed in by the judgment of what would seem to be a much lower court? The theology of the schools dissected the God who had revealed himself. Christian spirituality pressed God to its heart; the God who, as Father, had sent the eternal Son, and who had placed the eternal Spirit of love in the hearts of the faithful. The Spirit searches out the depths of the Godhead (are we able to join in the search?), and is bestowed upon us (1 Cor. 2, 11-16). Who would want to bar the way leading from Erigena to Eckhart and Nicholas of Cusa, and beyond them to Hegel? It began in a balance between a metaphysics that knows about the ineffable mystery and a theology that nevertheless is familiar with the mystery. It goes on to an all-encompassing metaphysics. Here the mystery is incorporated (in "Naturphilosophie"), as the preliminary contribution of antiquity, into an omniscient human wisdom which draws strength from Christianity and theology. But once the theological *a priori* in man's thinking is clearly seen, the theological gnosis is discredited, and faith is confined again within its (non-theoretical, existential) boundaries. The understanding is very cautious, like a burned child, about embarking on similar adventures. It is much more careful about establishing the bases of its positions, and has less to say than did the philosophy of antiquity.

This apparently puts Christian preaching in a precarious situation. From the 3rd century down to the 19th, Christianity formed an alliance with antiquity; and now this ally has had its weapons taken away. The Godward orientation of the thought of antiquity is now rejected as "mythological" and primitive by the enlightened understanding. Also, the theology that is tied up with this kind of philosophy is instructed to "de-mythologize" itself if it would be up to the standard of our age. Of course, a theology de-philosophized in this manner would have nothing more to do with the totality of being. Of necessity it could only present itself as a solace for the anguished "existential" subject.

One can see how endless are the complications involved in the theoretical question and yet how harshly practical are the consequences. Right and wrong are almost inextricably mixed. The question why there is anything at all is actually just as basic and

primary for man today as it was for men of all previous ages; and
no science—since science always begins its considerations with
what is already there—can relieve him of this question. If today
man does not pose the question, or, what comes to the same thing,
if he attempts to solve it through one of the particular sciences
(the science of matter, for example), the same "unforgivable"
sin and "darkening of the heart" (Rom. 1, 20-21) are imputed
to him as were imputed to Paul's contemporaries. The complicity
of Christianity with its gnostic familiarity with God and his mysteries (which is equivalent to a naïve forgetfulness of God) does
not justify the "unforgivable". Moreover, the alliance between
theology and philosophy (the philosophy of antiquity) is problematic. It is problematic not because Christianity took over the
vision of the invisible through the medium of the visible (in a
word, insight into the *analogy of being*), but rather because
Christianity did not see what was the limitation of philosophy, a
limitation that becomes apparent in theology. Thus Christianity
put itself in a false position relative to philosophy.

It is possible that by reconsidering these mistakes we may be
able to lead Christianity out of its present state of uncertainty
and pusillanimity.

II

What is philosophy's limitation? Nominalism or empiricism
would say that it is the impossibility of proceeding in the basic
metaphysical act beyond the individual existent toward the mystery of being. But nominalism and empiricism are mistaken.
From the pre-Socratics to Plotinus, philosophers have done just
this, and not without justification. This is the style that Nicholas
of Cusa termed "enigmatic" or "conjectural". There is nothing
specifically Christian about this approach to philosophy; it is
characteristic of humanity. Nor is the limit met when one attempts
this sort of thing subjectively (for basically it is the same sort of
thing), that is, when one ascends or returns from the limited subject to the unlimited subject, from the empirical to the intelligible

ego, whether this is done after the manner of Plato or of Marcus Aurelius, of Augustine or of Descartes, of Fichte or of Baader. And if Augustine speaks emphatically of the "noverim me, noverim te", and if repeatedly from Augustine to Newman the knowledge of "God and the soul" is considered to be the substance of the Christian's seeking, it should be pointed out that this emphasis can also take on the coloration of Platonism, Stoicism, or modern Idealism.

The relationship between God and the self becomes distinctively Christian only when God confronts the self as infinite and personal freedom; that is, only when God's definitive superiority to the *theion* of the all-encompassing being of ancient philosophy is asserted without the philosophically established affirmations about the *theion* becoming thereby superfluous. The personal exaltation of God, visible in Yahweh, only *seems* to entail what philosophically would be altogether impossible: the separation of God from the world. But in fact it guarantees a far more profound immanence, a presence and indwelling of God that is far more interior than was at all conceivable for the thought of antiquity. Philosophers (Spinoza, Hegel) have always been scandalized by the apparent removal of God through personal exaltation of this kind and this has prejudiced them against the Old Testament. God has let man, a thinking subject, see the exalted transcendence of the triune God of majesty and glory at the same time that he sees the immanence of God in all things, an immanence never repudiated but deepened instead.

However, it is this exalted transcendence of the free God that first brings his world into existence as *creation*. Let us be clear about this: the question why there is being or why a world exists at all becomes much more mysterious and non-rational in Christianity than it was for the "wisdom-loving Greeks". For the realm of ideas is no longer of any use in explaining existence. It does not even serve any more to explain the nature of essences. This tree is not a tree because there is an idea of a tree which it embodies. Now the question is: Who had the idea of a tree, whom did a tree occur to? Abstraction seems to take us a bit further, not only classifying but also differentiating the essential from the non-essential. But consider man. Whence the distinction between individuals? *Ratione materiae.* But with that, the far more formidable question is not yet posed: Whence the distinction and the juxtaposition of subjects? Here surely is the limit of all philosophy. One ego can distinguish itself from another only "accidentally". For this reason it goes on speaking only in general of the self, of the subject, of consciousness. It puts in brackets until the very end the question of how it is possible that one self-consciousness encounters "another" self-consciousness.

Questions in philosophical ethics concerning the relationships between men are never asked or answered except on the supposition that there is an identical human nature in every subject. So it was with Plato and the Stoics; so it was with the philosophy of the rights of man. And Kant quite logically derived the standard for our dealings with another person from an understanding of the depth and the value of the self. *Persona est philosophice ineffabilis, immo incogitabilis:* not the person "in general", but this "one of a kind" (though "kind" is false) and therefore irreplaceable person. Philosophy can only generalize by means of abstraction. Thus it develops a general anthropology, along with a general psychology (as the science of the relationships between individuals) and a general sociology (as the science of the relationships between groups); both of which all too easily let themselves be turned into what are called statistical sciences, in which the criterion and the goal is the nameless average man and the control of man from below (by chemical means, suggestion, propaganda, etc.).

It is impossible to establish philosophically, either in pre-Christian philosophy or in post-Christian idealism (to say nothing of materialism), that the individual person can possess an eternal and irreplaceable value. For example, what room does Fichte allow for a real meeting between an "I" and a "thou"? What is not the "I" is the "non-I", which has been projected for the "I" and which will be overcome by the "I". It is this that leads to Jean Paul Sartre's basic antipathy to Fichte's thought, similar to Herder's antipathy to Kant. In no philosophy is there a substructure for what is distinctively Christian. It makes no difference whether one constructs a philosophical anthropology after the manner of Plotinus, Thomas Aquinas, Nicholas of Cusa, or Fichte (as Maréchal and his followers do). All this "the heathens also do".

What is uniquely Christian begins and ends with the revelation that the infinite God loves the individual man infinitely. This is most exactly expressed by the fact that for this beloved "thou" God in human form died the death of a redeemer (that is, of a sinner). I come to know what I am, not from a universal *gnôthi sauton* and *noverim me,* but rather in consequence of Christ's deed. This tells me two things simultaneously: what I am worth to God, and how far I was from God. And Christ's deed is the proclamation of the eternal love of God, my Father, in that a fellowman, another person, has gone all the way in taking my place, has saved me by standing in my place, and has brought me back to be a child of God. My "I" is thus God's "thou", and can be an "I" only because God wishes to make himself my "thou"; and if this is the ultimate meaning of being and if, nevertheless, I am not to become the necessary fulfillment of God (an addition to God himself), then a final conclusion is unavoidable: God must in himself eternally be "I" and "thou" and the unity of both in love. The mystery of the Trinity is the irreducible prerequisite for the existence of a world. The mystery of the Trinity is required for the possibility of a drama of love *between* God and the world; it is required if this drama, as an encounter between "I" and "thou", is to fulfill the world's inner need.

An encounter of this kind is ontologically possible only if it entails the Christian fact, and thereby the entire Christian Dogmatics. Every encounter of this kind is an anamnesis of what God has done in Christ and a recapitulation in act of the Christian doctrine of God, Christology, ecclesiology, Mariology, and even the doctrine of the sacraments.[1] If the encounter takes place

[1] It is impossible to prove this here in detail, but the development of this theme could give a completely new rigor to dogmatic theology. Some indications of this can be found in my booklet, *Glaubhaft ist nur Liebe* (1963).

merely within the framework of that which "the heathen also do", then what we have is an encounter between instances of a common nature. These, operating within the framework of this nature, come to an agreement about morals (*ethos*), about the social order (*contrat social*), about the generally useful restrictions to be put on individual desire and egoism (as Hobbes realistically described it). In short, a compromise is reached, which may well provide that in case of necessity the individual (the model here is an animal colony) will be sacrificed for the good of the community, and that it is noble to make this sacrifice willingly (as do many heroes in the tragedies of Euripides). Between this and Christianity yawns an abyss. I first awaken to what it means to be a person by the fact that Jesus Christ takes me so seriously as a spiritual person that he gives his life for my eternal salvation, and by dying buries what was evil in me with himself in hell. "In this we have come to know his love, that he laid down his life for us; and we likewise ought to lay down (*opheilomen*) our life for the brethren" (1 John 3, 16).

But this is possible only if I understand myself as saved and borne along by Christ, and if I likewise see the "thou" whom I encounter as what in truth he is—as one eternally loved by God, one for whom God died, and one for whom I, too, am ready to give my life. If I am a Christian, I not only can, I *must* see Christ in my fellowman, and must see in Christ's deed the eternal love of God. And when I approach my fellowman with this vision and readiness, not only does he reveal Christ and God to me, but I reveal Christ and God to him. And this is not a lofty pinnacle for the elect; it is the one and only every-day commandment of Christ, which compels us constantly to encounter God in the most real way in our encounters with the other, the inconceivable "thou" whom the inconceivable God loves inconceivably. What takes place in this highest every-day manifestation of the faith of Christians is not only the ever-repeated experience of God among Christians; it is an ever-repeated and real witness of this experience of God before non-Christians. And if non-Christians complain that the cosmos no longer serves to bring them to God

—in our opinion because the cosmos is no longer ordered toward God but toward man as its meaning and goal—then they need only take their fellowmen seriously in the way in which they are taken seriously by (true) Christians, in order to have discovered the shortest, most compelling way to God.

This way, of course, cannot be traversed philosophically, for it is impossible philosophically to accord an eternal significance to the fleeting encounter of a finite, transitory "I" with a finite, transitory "thou". Consequently, philosophy cannot put on much of a show with this content of Christianity. What Christianity puts at the very center of things is so tiny when compared with the lordly systems of transcendental and evolutionary anthropology that it remains invisible even under a philosophical microscope. It depends upon God's eternal love for me—something which I would never even have dreamed of—and this God says and shows to me. The fact that the theological factor remains beyond the reach of philosophical discovery shows that God has chosen the "lower way", the "last place", in revealing himself. Relevation and the cross are identical, and Christian theology is nothing other than a calling attention to this lower way, this last place, this foolishness of God. But from this source shines all glory (*Kabod, Doxa, Gloria*), for every meaning that justifies "being" shines forth from out of the sheer gratuitousness of God's foolish love for the world.

In the Bible it is already the case that the glory of God in the universe is seen, understood, and praised to the extent that the glory of God is recognized in Sion. Cosmological revelation depends upon the history of salvation in order to become truly effective and to avoid the danger of turning the universe into a false good. In the same way, in the present moment in the history of the Church the responsibility for the effectiveness of the revelation of God in the universe is placed in the hands of Christians. Where the sign of salvation, love of man for man, shines brightly, the hieroglyphics of the book of the external world can, to some extent, be deciphered and God discovered. The more unmistakably the whole of Christianity orients itself toward the cross, the more it appropriates the wise foolishness of the cross and lets its presence shine forth—in deeds and not merely in words—the more theophanous will it make the world again.

It is humbling for us Christians that the philosopher who was the first, after the collapse of the great Western philosophical systems, to point out the simple Christian factor was an atheist (or something quite similar): Ludwig Feuerbach (*The Essence of Christianity*, 1841). Of course he did this in such a way that almost without noticing he went on to misconstrue and basically to misunderstand this. Still it remains to his credit that the reestablished the connection between the absoluteness of the Hegelian idea of God and the "I-thou" relationship. It is implied in it and is its proper expression. Only here is God visible, even though for Feuerbach this God is nothing other than the incomprehensible miracle of human love between the "I" and the "thou". We Christians must be prepared to see how non-Christians, too, are overcome by this miracle and give themselves up to its laws and its consequences, how they do this without perceiving all that this involves. Indeed, they do this in sharp and paradoxical contradiction to what seems to them to be philosophically evident about the world and man. Therefore, we must recognize the free working of the grace of Christ even where there is no explicit Christian belief. We must, to our shame, let others, perhaps atheists, give us an example of genuine self-giving. This humiliation is an essential part of our kerygma; through it the difference between "head" and "body", between the one redeemer and the denying followers, always remains clear to ourselves and to the world.

The Christian revelation has revealed aspects of God that are entirely hidden to philosophy. This includes God's incomprehensible freedom vis-à-vis the individual, as this is expressed in the doctrines of predestination, the efficacy of grace, and the final judgment with its possibility of condemnation. An echo of this incoercible freedom is the freedom which one meets in the "thou", which cannot be conceptualized from any philosophical standpoint (from the standpoint of a supra-individual, transcendental, intelligible ego, for instance). Only in contrast with a "thou" who is free in this way is the risk of total self-giving possible, self-giving of the kind that Christ has accomplished for me and for the "thou". I first see what "being" really is in the encounter with this free "other". I see that it is something which, in the technological idealism of the present age (for the *homo faber* imposes his forms on matter) I had come close to forgetting. Philosophy scents its prey here and stands ready to cast the broad mantle of its synthesis about the bare revelation (Origen, Nicholas of Cusa, Staudenmaier, Soloviev, Teilhard de Chardin: Plotinus is their common bond). Meanwhile, the incalculable love of God transcends man's gnosis. The syntheses of philosophy will be acceptable to the extent that they accommodate themselves to the inner form of the revelation of God's love, and promise no other certitudes than those of the "hope that does not deceive them".

Let us summarize briefly:

1. The invisible God, contemplated through his creation, is ontologically no more distant in our time than in any other.

2. Man's position in the cosmos as the transcending epitome of the world was basically already seen by the metaphysics of antiquity and by Christian metaphysics. The modern emphasis upon this view consequently does not affect our knowledge of God qualitatively.

3. Accidentally, the knowledge of God can today seem dimmed: (a) because we have been accustomed to a one-sided "downward view" of things, and because we are not accustomed to the efforts necessary for metaphysics; (b) because of a theoretical abuse of the revelation of God's love, an elimination of mystery—and this not without some share in the responsibility on the part of Christians.

4. The Christian revelation reveals to man who he is for God by showing him in Christ who God is for him. It thus places before him the true reality of being; this it does by constantly alerting him to being, in connection with the neighbor who is encountered, who is loved by God, and who is to be loved in God.

5. In this continual confrontation, a confrontation to which the principal Christian commandment compels the believer, the

believer must search for and find God in the neighbor and in this way recall and reveal God to him. All dogmatic propositions are implicit in this experience.

6. Encounter, in the simple carrying out of Christian responsibility, is the "sacrament" in which God wills "to be among us" in an almost-experiential way. This encounter is also the center from which the cosmos, with all its miracles, laws, and terrors, becomes theophanous.

Karl Rahner, S.J./*Munich, W. Germany*

Christianity and Ideology

The last session of the Council has brought us to an awareness of the Church's relation to the contemporary world, a theme, which like no other, has stirred up the deepest attention in the widest circles, a theme, moreover, beyond any other in its complexity and number of presuppositions. But behind every discussion of this theme there lurks a question that is always involved at least implicitly, a question constantly raised and argued, the question, namely, of the relation of the faith, or more generally, of Christianity, to ideology. The following reflections will attempt to deal with this question.

By way of proceeding, let us first define what we mean by "ideology", for we cannot assume that this term is so univocal and so commonly understood as to be taken for granted. Then we will investigate briefly the reasons for considering Christianity as an ideology and for rejecting it as such; we will show how Christianity is not an ideology, and that it cannot therefore be rejected on this score. In the last part of our consideration, we will deduce a few corollaries from the basic thesis of the third part.

I

WHAT IS "IDEOLOGY"?

What, then, do we mean by "ideology" in this discussion? This is not the place to examine the origin and history of the term.

In fact, historically, the term has been used so inconsistently that at best all we can hope to do here is to define our own usage, alluding to the historical usages as reference points, whenever that is useful. But for all that, the definition to be developed here is not arbitrary, but rather one that philosophically conforms to the subject itself. Let us say at once, then, that by ideology, in the negative sense we intend, we mean an erroneous system that must be rejected by a true interpretation of reality. We are not concerned now with the question whether these false systems occur outright as fully developed theories or as unreflexive attitudes of the mind, or as arbitrary and voluntaristic moods. In fact, the question is left open just where we would find an ideology in our sense, whether, for instance, every metaphysics might not be understood as such an ideology. What interests us here, apart from the obvious errors that characterize all ideologies, has more to do with the very essence of an ideology, namely, the way all ideologies set themselves up as *total* systems by willfully slamming the door, so to speak, on reality as a whole; in more customary language this is spoken of as absolutizing a partial aspect of reality. We should broaden this definition by adding that this absolutizing of a partial aspect of reality, insofar as it may claim men's assent, occurs in connection with practical matters and for that reason is usually found as the basis for political action and ultimately as the rule of social life. From this we may appreciate the fittingness of Lauth's definition of ideology as a pseudo-scientific interpretation of reality in the service of some political, social end which in its turn legitimizes the ideology.

From our formal definition of ideology as a kind of closing off, an absolutizing of a part of reality, it would seem that three possible forms of ideology suggest themselves *a priori*. This is not to say, we must add, that these forms are ever going to be wholly realized purely and simply as such. There is, then, an ideology of immanence, an ideology of transmanence, and an ideology of transcendence. These divisions may be explained briefly as follows:

1. In the ideology of immanence, specific, limited regions of

our total experience are absolutized and made to be the rule and law for all reality. This group includes the greater part of what we usually refer to as ideologies: nationalism, blood and soil, ideologies of race, Americanism, technologism, socialism, and of course that materialism for which such words as God, spirit, freedom, and person in their true sense are but empty phrases.

2. As a counterpart—although it is seldom seen this way—to this ideology of immanence, the ideology of transmanence embraces such systems as supernaturalism, quietism, certain forms of utopianism, Chiliasm, indiscrete "fraternalism", and so on. In this kind of ideology what is ultimate, infinite and pervasive of all spheres of reality is absolutized (or better still: totalized) in such a way that the penultimate and finite, the things always given and assumed in immediate experience are not given their due and are overlooked. If anything, they are manipulated by projections from that absolute vision of the mind—a failing to which philosophers and religious men are particularly susceptible.

3. The third form of ideology, the ideology of transcendence, seeks to overcome the first two forms of ideology that we enumerated and to hypostatize its purely formal victory over their claims to validity. This form of ideology shuns the data of immediate experience through historicism and relativism, etc., and looks upon the transcendent in its true nature as something elusive and unutterable. Thus, this ideology advocates a program of so-called boundless openness to everything in general together with a scrupulous avoidance of a straightforward commitment to anything in particular. One can also see from this how this attitude, which is peculiarly and recognizably Western, could be set against the claims of an "Eastern" ideology, and why it is that Communism, with its "engagement" ever and again exercises a seductive power over Western intellectuals.

II

Is Christianity an Ideology?

The reproach is often made that Christianity, too, is merely an ideology in this negative sense. Before we consider why such a reproach is unjust, we need to ask ourselves briefly what could be the reasons that would appear to justify this interpretation of Christianity.

The reproach that Christianity is an ideology could very well seem legitimate to someone who refused to reflect on the matter at all, or who expressly held a consistently skeptical, relativistic view of things. Whenever experience, for personal or cultural reasons, is automatically identified with the kind of reality which technology and the natural sciences can demonstrate; whenever every other reality and experience is felt to be a freely exchangeable, *i.e.*, ideological superstructure upon the true reality of exact empiricism, or is so devalued; whenever metaphysics, because of the undemonstrable nature of its subject, is devalued as a mere opinion or a plain conceptual figment by an experience which, to begin with, has been confined to the empirical sciences, Christianity, to be sure, will inevitably be seen as an ideology. It would not make any difference, either, how the origin of this ideology were explained, whether as the opium of the people, as the product of a particular social condition, as a utopian dream for human existence, or as the effect of the basic need for an all-inclusive interpretation of reality.

A further ground for the interpretation of Christianity as an ideology is found in the historical fact that Christianity has actually often been misused, sometimes for revolutionary purposes, but, for the most part in conservative, reactionary ways as a means of justifying a social, economic, political, cultural, or scientific condition, which can claim no permanent reality. To be sure, such a misuse of Christianity is difficult to avoid and for the most part is only overcome gradually by the slow processes of history; but where such a misuse has been made, Christianity is indeed changed into an ideology, and not infrequently this conservative ideology bearing the name of Christianity has been quite rightly combated precisely *as* ideology. If true Christianity itself has had to suffer in this struggle, this was the fault or the tragic misfortune of the representatives of Christianity and the Church who brought it about, since they themselves provided the occasion for this misunderstanding of Christianity as an ideology which was to be overcome.

The need for objectivizations of Christianity's essence presents a greater and more subtle ground for this danger that Christianity will be mistaken for an ideology—the need to objectivize the inscrutable mystery of God who is above the world and his salvation through an absolute giving of himself for our pardon categorically, historically, institutionally, sacramentally, and legalistically, revelation in human words, in sacramental signs, and in social organizations of the believers. These objectivizations of God's own divine self-giving, which seizes man at his transcendental source, are necessitated by the fact that man must live out his original nature and his eternal destiny as an historical being in time and space, and cannot discover his true nature in pure inwardness, in mysticism, and in the simple dismissal of his historical being.

These objectivizations are necessary; they are the body in which the spirit finds and realizes itself. They, however, necessarily veil the true object of Christianity, making it somewhat equivocal and to that extent expose it to misuse and unduly narrow interpretations. As ideology of immanence they are apt, especially in the case of fervent Christians, to provide the tempation to the ideologies of transmanence and transcendence to regard themselves as the true reflection of Christianity's essence, thus further exposing Christianity to the accusation of being itself an ideology.

Another basis for this danger is given in the pluralistic world outlook which is so prevalent today, and which, moreover, underlies the skeptical relativism given as the first reason for this confusion of Christianity with ideology. If man today, formed as he is by the natural sciences, assumes the universal validity of truth as a self-evident ideal and norm, and if he is basically inclined in his democratic view of things to attribute to others as much intelligence and goodwill as he attributes to himself, then he cannot help but be struck and dismayed by the fact that the various outlooks people have, the interpretations they give to their own being in the world, are so utterly lacking in unity. Such a person would be in danger of concluding from this fact that any understanding, which ventures beyond the strict realm of the natural sciences and generally acknowledged cognitions, is a loose fabrication of ideas which possess subjective significance at most. And he will be tempted to include Christianity—just because it is so controverted—among such subjective, poetic ideas, conceding at most that it has a more profound subjective affinity for us.

III

WHY CHRISTIANITY IS NOT AN IDEOLOGY

These in rough outline are the reasons for the assessment of Christianity as an ideology, which brings us to the third part of our reflection, to the central question of why Christianity is *not* an ideology. To answer this question adequately, we would first have to establish the justice of Christianity's claim that it sets forth the truth about the whole of reality and that it is the absolute religion, or (if one shies away from the word religion) that it accomplishes what the religions of men vainly seek to accomplish of themselves. It is clear, of course, that a demonstration of this kind would require too much discussion and could not be offered here. There would have to be an account, for instance, of what in such a connection, truth and absolute validity really mean. The question would have to be asked whether man finds access to God and to his revealed Word at all; how the Christian message as the efficacious Word of God proves itself to man's sense for truth; what is really affirmed in this message and what is not affirmed; what does image, symbol, and cipher signify in this message; what does it intend to teach, what is its reality and truth?

It is obvious that these and many other necessary questions cannot be answered here. All we can hope to do here is to stress a few of the highlights of Christianity as it relates to ideology, whereby Christianity can be differentiated from that which in a false, erroneous system is especially signified and emphasized by the word "ideology". What follows, then, will be seen in the light of this restriction.

First, the charge that Christianity is an ideology is inadmissible from the fact that Christianity makes absolute assertions which claim to be true in the pure and simple meaning of that word. These assertions can be called "metaphysical", since on the one hand they are made with an absolute claim to truth, and on the other hand, the validity of this claim cannot be directly demonstrated in the empirical world of the natural sciences. Of course, anyone who regards all metaphysics as false or undemonstrable will obviously look upon authentic Christianity, in its very own understanding of itself, as an ideology. He may then perhaps go on to reflect in a mood of existential irrationalism how this Christianity still holds an essential meaning for his life. What he does not realize, to be sure, is that such a reflection, as an irrational conception and ideologizing of life, is itself metaphysics, even if a bad one. This does not mean, of course, that faith and metaphysics, in their basic structures, are the same or that they are differentiated only with regard to their stated objects. But the Christian faith and metaphysics do agree with respect to the claim each makes to truth. So that if the possibility of a metaphysical affirmation is disputed on principle and *a priori,* then Christianity, too, will have to be accorded only the status of a subjective ideology because in this view there is no subject that can claim absolute truth—there are only isolated individuals trying to make their lives more bearable and noble through some such poetic idea.

To defend Christianity from the charge that it is an ideology, we must stress that metaphysics, by its definition, cannot under any circumstances be regarded as an ideology. The truth of this is already shown from the fact that in the last analysis, the proposition, *every metaphysics is an ideology,* is itself a metaphysical proposition, whether it is stated as a theoretically gratuitous argument or is implied in an attempt to live a life free of metaphysics (in a radically skeptical attempt at "bracketing" any going beyond the brutal experiences of life and the knowledge of natural science). Relativism and skepticism are themselves metaphysical decisions whether theoretically formulated or untheoretically attempted in life. Metaphysics is inevitably given with man's existence; man invariably interprets his experience from a previously established and comprehensive context of *a priori* judgments. Genuine metaphysics, however, consists of reflections on those transcendental and irrefusable implications which carry in themselves their own light and certainty and which of necessity are present in a free, spiritual actualization of existence.

Inasmuch as metaphysics, as reflective understanding, does not originate these implications, but only reflects on what is always given, making them thematic—and for that reason may be spoken of as the thematisizing of transcendental experience, which as the unthematic ground of every empirical experience and understanding of truth on principle surpasses them in rationality and certitude—metaphysics can acknowledge with equanimity the incompleteness and unexclusiveness of its reflections, the ever recurrent need to begin anew, and yet still be able to say with confidence that its object, the transcendental experience itself, is still the common good of men who are open to the truth. This can be seen as such even in the plurality of metaphysical systems, when to the untutored eye and to bad philosophers of history these systems simply appear contradictory, and so create an impression of arbitrariness and subjectivity, a poetry of ideas.

Only by closing the mind completely and by living in what amounts to an animal immediacy with one's biological being, unaware of one's metaphysical *epoché* and unable to realize it, could a person be said to be free of metaphysics and able to escape any pretension to absolute truth. But if a metaphysics, which cannot be disposed of *a priori* as ideology, is at least in principle possible, then neither can Christianity be rejected, since the sphere of the affirmations of the faith does not coincide with that of the primitive, objective experiences of daily life or the empiricism of the natural sciences. The mere existence of philosophical pluralism then, is no valid reason for disposing of every view of the world as an ideology (so far as one includes metaphysics and the teaching of the Christian faith among these world views). For this attitude itself would affect the individual objects of empirical experience and their functional relations in such a way as to convert experience as such—which is never the object of experience—into the object of an affirmation, which, by this very definition would be an ideology.

A right approach to the pluralism in metaphysics and in philosophy in general must consist not in having blanket misgivings about them, looking upon them as mythologies, but in preserving an attitude which painstakingly examines everything, keeping itself open to new understanding and to modifications of previous understanding, modestly trying to discover the transcendental experience common to all the systems that are offered, but which also then has the courage to come to a decision, to acknowledge with calm certitude that absolute truth is being attained in an historically determined, finite, incomplete and open-ended statement, even if this in the last analysis is that holy and unutterable mystery which cannot be fitted into a higher order, subject to our disposal.

If metaphysics is understood as a rational, or still better, as a spiritual induction into this attitude of openness to the absolute mystery, which always lives on the ground of our spiritual, free and responsible being (which, because of that, man dare not take for granted) then metaphysics loses its appearance of ideological poetry even in confrontation with all the pluralistic views of the world today. The pluralism of world views adversely affects only the rationalistic presumption of a false metaphysics, *i.e.,* that man seizes the totality of reality in its ultimate ground and masters it in his own system, instead of being himself seized by it and struck dumb before the ground of reality's wholeness, both in his life and in his reflections on the implications of this mystery.

There is a still further reason why Christianity is not an

ideology. We have already stated that the basis for all metaphysically valid understanding of truth is the transcendental experience by which man, for the sake of concrete, individual experience, is already previously turned to the incomprehensible wholeness of reality at its very center: that holy mystery, always present,
which confronts man with the distance in his finiteness and guilt,
and which we call God. This transcendental experience which
penetrates our understanding and our freedom as the unthematic
ground and horizon of our everyday experiences, as the very condition of their possibility, is the primary "locus" of Christianity,
without prejudice for Christianity's history or its historicity, as we
shall show later. Because this experience of transcendence, this
induction into an absolute and holy mystery which we cannot
seize but which seizes us instead, by its own transcendental necessity, transcends ideologies which absolutize limited regions of experience and because Christianity in its reality signifies just exactly
this transcendental experience itself, and in its teaching represents
the right interpretation of this transcendental experience in its
true and unabridged essence, then for this very reason, Christianity cannot be an ideology. And if the reality of Christianity is
what Christians customarily call grace; if grace is the self-communication of God to the finite creature and the creature's immediacy to God, the dynamic participation in God's life as a
creature raised above everything finite and mortal; if grace signifies that man in spite of his finiteness and guilt is raised above the
forces and powers of this world even as he suffers and endures
them; if this grace because of God's will to save all mankind is at
work in everyone (even where man resists it of his own volition):
then all this means that man, in the ground of his personal being,
is borne by God himself and is drawn into an intimacy with him.

By grace, then, we mean the real truth and divinely given reality of the transcendental experience of the personal spirit's
openness toward God. So then if Christianity by its very nature is
grace, *i.e.,* the innermost possibility and reality of receiving God's
self-communication into the ground of our being, then Christianity is nothing less than the purest actuality of that transcendental

experience, the experience of the absolute and forgiving nearness of God himself. And this nearness is differentiated from the reality of this world, is exalted above it, and for that reason remains the holy, adorable mystery (also and even especially in this absolute presence).

If this is the true nature of Christianity, then Christianity exists on an altogether different plane than ideology. For each ideology wants to deal with the data of experience in the world, whether this is blood and soil, society, rational technologization and manipulation, the pleasures of life, or the experience of true emptiness and absurdity, etc., and takes these as the fundamental determinants of life. Christianity, on the other hand, explains these powers and forces, the masters of unredeemed existence, as false gods, unworthy to be our masters, and explains that by God's grace man has already subdued these powers and forces in the ground of his being. The only issue now is whether or not man cooperates with grace by giving his free consent to his transcendental openness to the immediacy of the God of eternal life, which consent is likewise given by the power of this grace. Because Christianity is achieved from the very center of man's transcendentality, which very precisely as a transcendence to the mystery of God's absolute, forgiving presence rises above ideologies of this world, Christianity by definition cannot be an ideology; at least, not an ideology of immanence. And since this transcendence is not extrinsic but is intrinsic to man's being, not a dimension superadded to his life in the world but rather as the ground condition for its possibility, then Christianity cannot be considered as a later and superfluous ideologizing of man's life.

Christianity is also essentially history, however; it is man turned to events fixed by time and space in human history as events of salvation, a history which has its climax in the absolute event of salvation, Jesus Christ, who is both the center and the measure of history. This history itself belongs to the very essence of Christianity; it is not just a loose collection of agreeable recollections about the transcendental experience of the grace of the absolute, forgiving presence of the holy mystery, as the overcoming of the powers and forces of this world. That is why Christianity appears as an unmistakable "no" to every ideology of transmanence and transcendence—not, let it be understood, as the undoing of transcendence, but as the undoing of the ideologization of transcendence, the barren formalization of true transcendence.

Two things should be understood at this point. First, the intrinsic connection between the genuine, unexcelled historicity of Christianity as a turning to real events of salvation in history, and the transcendental nature of Christianity as the grace of openness to the absolute God must be made abundantly clear. It must be shown, therefore, that true transcendentality and true historicity mutually condition each other, and that man by his transcendentality is referred to a real history that he cannot dismiss by an *a priori* judgment. Secondly, it must be understood that man in his burden of actual history is obligated and empowered to take his *secular* existence with utmost seriousness and to be engaged in the historical even where the recognition and experience of the contingency and relativity of the historical is most painful. The right understanding of man's history is not that it is an accident which has been imposed as an additional burden on his transcendental nature, but that it is the history precisely of his transcendental nature as such. Man lives his existence toward God, not in a pure, quasi-mystical inwardness in depths beyond the reach of history, but rather in the very history of his being, both individual and collective. Hence, Christianity can be the condition of grace for man's transcendental nature and still be truly history, in which this nature realizes itself and in the objectivity of space and time encounters man himself.

This is why there is true history of salvation of the human word together with the Word of God which is given through it, and a Church which is both the community of salvation and Sacrament, even though all these historical objectivizations drawn by God's grace from the absolute depths of man's nature realize their true nature—something which is true for all historical manifestations—as mediations and signs of God's incomprehensibility, who shares himself with man through an absolute forgiving immediacy in all truth and reality. As long as these historical mediations, therefore, manifest the mystery of God's presence and acceptance, they preserve their relationship, and as long as (before the immediate vision of God) they prove to be indispensable for man's historical nature, then history and transcendence are inseparable; and Christianity for this reason could not be made out as an ideology of immanence, which idolizes the powers of this world, nor as ideology of transmanence and transcendence, which idolize man's grace-filled transcendentality into empty, formal abstractions.

Two further points must be made in this connection. First, man's historicity, understood as the mediation to his transcendental nature, elevated by grace, finds its culmination in Jesus Christ, the God-Man. In him God's promises of himself to the world are realized, and in such a way that this mediation and its acceptance by man in history are inseparably joined without becoming confused; God's historically unexcellable eschatological mediation to himself is given through the history of grace in the world, without this mediation ever becoming identified with God himself as the Monophysites have done. Man must accept this mediation through God's immediacy as something irreplaceable, receiving it humbly in his own grace-filled transcendentality as a purely contingent provision of history.

Man's relationship with this historical mediation of grace to the ground of his being is not established by a purely theoretical, historical knowledge of these saving events in history, a knowledge that could be suspected of being an ideology, but by a direct, realistic, utterly untheoretical process of knowing, achieved through the living unity of the history of salvation, through the Church (which is more than the sum of theoretical accord), through Sacrament and cult, through what we call anamnesis, tradition, etc. Because this mediation to the historical events of salvation occurs not through a theoretical process of knowing but as an event of man's own grace-filled transcendental nature, he is completely outside the arena of the three basic forms of ideology which we have been discussing.

The second point to consider is that the Christian, aware of his need for this historical mediation of grace, can and must take his "secular" history with perfect seriousness, too. To be sure, he does not absolutize it into an ideology, but he sees this history as the concrete expression of God's will who in his freedom brings forth the events of history as conditioned and contingent, in contrast to his own nature, and who endows them with the seriousness of a situation in which eternal destinies are decided before God. How history can be taken so seriously and not be ideologized will be discussed later.

One last point remains to be stressed against the thesis that Christianity is an ideology. Ideologies mutually exclude each other in their teaching and intention; and in fact this warfare and mutual contradiction are what ideologies are made of; what they have in common, as it were, exists despite their ideological theories and not because of them. Christianity, on the other hand, acknowledges an aspect of its faith which we will call "anonymous Christianity". It does not restrict the reality of its forgiving and divinizing grace to the circle of those who profess its categorical, historical, didactic objectivations, its expressly Christian teachings and their bearer, the Church. Instead, Christianity, bearing in mind God's holy will and the possibility of justification through the Sacrament, incorporates its adversaries into its own reality and accordingly can hardly regard them as adversaries in the same sense as ideologies necessarily regard them. Of course, ideologies may still accept their adversaries out of a certain tolerance (which is not completely reconcilable with the nature of an ideology) because they are people, or because they otherwise have some neutral ground in common. But that one's own positively intended and specific position should be acknowledged also in the antagonist on the deeper level of theoretical reflection and social existence, this, no ideology can concede because no ideology can acknowledge a third power outside of itself which transcends explicit differences and is able thereby to re-establish a common reality. Ideologies can never be bigger than themselves; Christianity on the other hand is bigger than itself because it is the movement of man's abandonment to this indisponible mystery, in the knowledge that this movement will bring him into the saving presence of this mystery, Jesus Christ.

IV

COROLLARIES

We should add to these reflections on why Christianity is not an ideology, a few corollaries that follow from our thesis.

1. Christianity is not an ideology. From its nature and from the teachings about its own special reality, certain universal norms of action are given by which man conforms himself to God, even in secular matters, norms which in the end will bring man to a renewed openness to God's absolute, forgiving presence in *all* the dimensions of human existence. We ought not to confine the faith, therefore, to any particular dimension; rather we should see it as the inner law of our whole life. These universal norms, however, insofar as they are contained in the Christian message and are proclaimed in the teaching ministry of the Church, leave ample room for imperatives and programs that are conditioned by the situations in history. This gives rise to several considerations. On the one hand, the Church as such cannot become the direct, official bearer, as it were, of the concrete imperatives and programs, *i.e.,* the concrete archetypal patterns for the shaping of history. She cannot tell the Christian in his individual and collective history exactly what he must do here and now. She cannot take from him the burden of hazardous, historical decisions, and their possible frustration, nor can she spare him the fact that history ever and again turns into blind alleys. The Church must, therefore, refuse to become an ideology, if we mean by this an historical program which has to regard itself as absolute in order to carry any historical weight.

The refusal of the Church to become an ideology in this sense, however, does not mean that the Christian, in his individual and collective decisions here and now, does not have the obligation by virtue of his Christian responsibility to choose a particular, concrete imperative and thereby to take upon himself the burden and risk of putting such an imperative into practice. If his transcendental Christian nature is to be realized in his historical being in *all* its dimensions, then it becomes necessary and obligatory for him to find a concrete imperative for the affairs of history, deriving from the very center of his Christian existence, even though the Church as such cannot supply it. He accepts this Christian responsibility for concrete decisions in his historical situation, but he accepts it in earnest obedience to the absolutely binding will of the Living God, and therefore he does not ideologize these decisions. This is possible for the Christian because without falling into quietism or skepticism, without relativizing his conduct, he secures his decisions more and more deeply in the decrees of the absolute sovereign Lord of reality, by whose grace the outcome and the risk of this decision become secure and salvific, who is able to demand and render possible for other times other decisions which conform to his will.

2. If Christianity is not an ideology, if the imperatives and the concrete decisions attendant upon the attitudes and affairs of this world, which the Christian can and must make, are not to be ideologized, then tolerance is necessary to the Christian; tolerance as an expression of the need to avoid particular ideologies in the Church. Such tolerance is necessary to him because we cannot expect that all Christians will come to this choice of a concrete imperative, to this interpretation of the historical hour and to a decision on a definitive historical course all in the same way.

Strife among such varied decisions will certainly be unavoidable, even for Christians. Nor could it be avoided by theoretical discussions, since such discussions would assume basically that the concrete imperative for the here and now could be derived univocally from universal principles and from a purely static, neutral analysis of the given situation. This would be, however, a rationalistic error, since each decision for some concrete action adds to our *a priori* knowledge of essence, an irreducible element, the choice, namely, of a single existence among many that are possible. Just because strife, the concurrence of real opposing tendencies in regard to performance is unavoidable beyond the purely theoretical level, both the Christian and the Church need what we mean by tolerance: sympathy for the position of the other, fairness in battle—that singular unity of decision with which one defends one's own position (but for all that, fair, even when waged in earnest)—and the readiness to allow oneself to be overruled and to remain within the wholeness of the Church when the decisions of the Church go contrary to one's own.

From what was said previously about anonymous Christianity as the refusal to regard Christianity as an ideology, it would follow that a similar attitude of positive tolerance toward the non-Christian is also appropriate, a tolerance which distinguishes the firmness and missionary zeal of the believer from fanaticism. The latter is peculiarly a trait of ideology, for only through such fanaticism can ideology, with its limitations, be sure of itself against the fuller reality which surrounds it. Christianity, however, by its very nature, is called to seek itself in the other, and to trust that in the other it encounters itself again in a greater abundance.

3. Christianity must, of course, constantly be on guard against the danger of misunderstanding itself as an ideology. It makes no difference whether this would occur as an ideology of transmanence, as an ideology of transcendence, or whether a particular attitude and decision valid for some special circumstance and adopted practically for the moment throughout Christendom becomes absolutized and hardened into a particular, reactionary ideology. Christianity is not preserved from such dangers simply as a matter of course, and it cannot be said that it has never lapsed into them. All that is merely doctrinaire and institutional as such, offers by itself no guarantee against such ideological hardening, especially since one can in turn absolutize the protest against the former into an empty ideology. The Christian has solely the trust that the pure and indisponible grace of God will not fail to ward off this danger.

Christians may disagree as to where God's victorious grace is concretely situated in his Church, or what its nature is, that this

grace in his Church preserves and rescues us from the absoluti-
zations of ideology. But in their trust in this grace itself, Christians are one. Grace is always also the grace of preservation from
ideology, which in the end is nothing more than the absolutizing
of man by his own means.

Johannes B. Metz/*Münster, W. Germany*

Unbelief as a Theological Problem

The problem of unbelief is no doubt one of the most pressing and difficult questions raised in Vatican Council II by Schema XIII, entitled, "The Church in the Modern World". Since this problem of unbelief is extremely complex, a future volume of this section will be totally dedicated to it. Therefore this article will limit its treatment to only one of its aspects. It will consider unbelief insofar as it is a problem of the *believer's* very faith and existence in the Church.

I

The question of unbelief is undergoing a special transposition in present-day theological thought. It is passing from being a borderline question within an apologetical defense of belief or within a confrontation with other philosophical views of life, to being a central question of theology itself, where the importance and seriousness of its problematic can become manifest. The reason why this question of unbelief is being seen as the more basic question of belief itself and as a theological question is not without reason due to the embarrassment encountered by the direct apologetic of belief when faced with present-day unbelief, because this unbelief has not only ceased to be the esoteric privilege of the sophisticated, but it has become the spiritual attitude of many people. Above all, it has ceased more or less to be a "direct unbelief" involving the explicit negation of belief. It is no longer a world view or a philosophy of life *in opposition to God,* but rather the presentation of a positive possibility of existence *without God.* Today, this thematic atheism is not really the object of unbelief, but rather its presupposition.[1]

This a-religious and not anti-religious unbelief offers no point of contact with direct apologetics. There seems to be no immediate object for such a confrontation. Hence, recent attempts of Catholic theology to deal with this phenomenon of contemporary unbelief and to answer it from the responsibility imposed by belief, constitute a search for a way of "indirect apologetic", so to speak. These theologians seek to uncover the implicit belief of the unbeliever, the belief he professes despite his consciously avowed statements. By this very approach the question about unbelief becomes a question of the self-understanding of belief. For belief is thus taken somewhat in the sense of *fides implicita* which can be actually present in those who explicitly reject it or make its rejection the presupposition of the meaning of their life.

In consideration of the facts of our faith, *i.e.,* God's universal will of salvation and his offer of grace to all, theologians try to develop a concept of belief that would make room for implicit or anonymous belief on the part of the unbeliever. These reflections and arguments are indeed important and indispensable;[2] they acknowledge the question about unbelief as an inner theological question. Yet, we must ask whether this has established the ultimate theological place and status of the question about unbelief, which would give legitimacy, measure, credibility and

---

[1] B. J. Lacroix, *Le sens de l'Athéisme moderne* (Paris, 1958). The roots of this a-religious self-understanding of unbelief go back to Feuerbach and Marx, and their search for a "real humanism": Feuerbach absolutizes the human interpersonal relations (of love), while Marx absolutizes in the same sense human society at large as the basis for the definitive and autonomous humanization of man.

[2] We find these thoughts in H. de Lubac (those who feel that they cannot believe), in Karl Rahner (the anonymous Christian), recently also in Schillebeeckx (implicit Christianity).

pathos to every form of apologetic concern with the actual unbelief of today. It seems to me that the question about unbelief must be located yet more deeply in the self-understanding of belief, and its inner theological origin must be proved still more decisively. The unfolding of this modest perspective of an extremely differentiated problem implicating the whole of theology shall be the subject of the subsequent reflections. The ecclesiological aspect of the theme, namely, the specific ecclesial place of the problem of unbelief which includes the question of the nature of the Church, cannot be considered here.

This "apologetical" concern rightly understood and seen from this limited perspective has been formulated by Jean Lacroix in his book, *Le sens de l'Athéisme moderne*:[3] a certain kind of apologetic appears to have recently overstressed the implicit belief of the unbeliever and asserted his belief in God—against himself. Today we should have to emphasize more the unbelief of the believer. And we may add, only when the question is given this fundamental turn can it creditably become a question about the belief of the unbeliever. The expression "the unbelief of the believer" is probably not new. But has it been taken seriously in all its consequences? Has it been thought out and given an exact foundation in Catholic doctrine concerning the nature of faith and in Catholic fundamental theology, which considers itself more and more as a strictly theological discipline and tries to give its answers from a responsibility immanent in the faith (cf. 1 Peter 3, 15)?

If unbelief had been analyzed sufficiently as a theological problem, whence would come the strange hiddenness of unbelief *in* theology? Where is discussed not merely the lack of authenticity of the Christian's belief but the very unbelief itself in the believer? Where in the analysis of faith is unbelief discussed? The situation seems to be this. Either unbelief is dealt with as an inner theological problem, as part of the general doctrine of sin and for this very reason its radical nature remains hidden because it is

[3] J. Lacroix, *op. cit.*

seen only as a particular sin and not as the problematic of belief
in quantum est radix et fundamentum omnis justificationis.[4] Or,
again, unbelief is taken mainly as an object of purely apologetical
considerations *ad extra*. But does unbelief really touch the believer only as a missionary problem? as an external threat to his
own life of faith? only insofar as unbelief narrows the sociological
basis of the believers and seems to render more and more relative
the claim to the universality and absoluteness of the faith of the
believers? Is unbelief a concern of the believer only insofar as he
has to be a witness to God's universal will of salvation before the
world and is to proclaim the message of the faith "to the end of
the world", only insofar as the genuine concern for the salvation
of the unbeliever is a test of the believer's own faith?

In all these alternatives unbelief is and remains always the unbelief of "the other"; it is unbelief *extra nos*. Unbelief, however,
affects the believer more basically and inescapably in his own act
of faith and in the subjectivity of his own faith[5]—as unbelief of
the believer, as unbelief *intra nos*. Only if unbelief is seen in this
way and if the question concerning the possibility of faith in the
unbeliever is posed as the possibility of unbelief in the believer,
can the fundamental inner theological place be revealed from
which as a vantage point we can obtain a creditable attitude toward unbelief *extra nos*.

II

Theologically, it is possible to show two phases of the implication of unbelief in the believer.

1. There is a general and lasting danger to belief which is not
a later and external result of some historical accident, but which
comes from, and belongs to, its very nature.

This essential danger shines forth from the central theological

---

[4] Denz. 801, 178, 200 b, 1789, 1793.

[5] Or better: intersubjectivity of faith. The act of faith never occurs as an
act of monadic existence but in every case and essentially in union
(*Mitsein*) with others; and this because it is the most "personal" and most
"existential" determination of the individual existence. Cf. our later reference to intersubjectivity.

statement that belief is singularly a *free and imponderable gift of grace according to divine predestination*. Never is belief a static property *in* man, much less his disponible possession. The believer has at no time existentially acquired his belief once and for all; it lies ever and again before him as a possibility of his existence, to be received as a free gift freely coming anew (*Zukunft*) from God. Only misunderstanding of grace as a thing-like object could give the impression that the doctrine of faith as a *habitus infusus* denies the essentially (*unaufhebbar*) actual dependence of belief on God's free and imponderable grace. The *habitus* of faith is forever subject to God's free disposition; it "hovers so to speak on the point of God's free grace and on the point of the freedom of man" [6] whose assent itself is again the more powerful act of God, thus depending in its very origin on the prevenience of his grace. This hovering actuality of our faith cannot be firmly stabilized by recourse to God's universal will of salvation since it involves the effective event of the *individual* belief *of each one* of us.[7] This characteristic of our faith, namely, of being beyond our power of disposition, which can never be solidified into a thing-like condition, justifies and emphatically demands that we consider our faith as a radically precarious and endangered possession.

This first phase of the implication of unbelief in the believer stands out yet more clearly when we consider the anthropological determinations of faith indicated by the theological *analysis fidei*. One determination seems to us essentially relevant: the determination of faith as a *free* act. The act of faith involves the highest freedom.[8]

Belief is something incomprehensible and awesome, qualities

[6] K. Rahner, "Gerecht und Sünder zugleich" (At the same time just and sinner), in *Geist und Leben* 36 (1963), pp. 434-43 (citation 441).

[7] Unless this "universality" of the fidelity of God was taken not in a simply abstract-essentialistic sense, but as the fidelity which I believe for the others—the brethren—due to the essentially human interrelationship of my belief. In this way the fidelity of God attains a true existential universality without ceasing to be a special fidelity to the individual.

[8] *E.g.*, J. B. Metz, "Freiheit als philosophisch-theologisches Grenzproblem," in *Gott in Welt* I (Freiburg, 1964), pp. 287-314.

that are proper to our freedom. They reveal themselves as such by the fact that our freedom is so intimately part of ourselves that it cannot be replaced or discarded. Neither can it be fully grasped by reflection and hence cannot be consciously controlled in our existence. The believer can never be certain of his fundamental option in faith because freedom is its formative element. Conscience in which belief knows about itself is lastly always somewhat reluctant and forbidding. It is not knowledge by which the believer can once more rise powerfully above himself, but rather an innocent sort of knowledge. The truth of this knowledge is not revealed to the believer by a backward glance at himself and at his subjective act of faith in another attempt to ascertain this act of faith. It is rather a knowledge that only results from forgetting self in placing ever new acts of faith, *i.e.,* it is the knowledge of the believer "doing the truth" (John 3, 21). His free subjective faith has the awesomeness of a face without a mirror.

Faith, thus withdrawn from the judgment of the believer, is being experienced as a faith that ultimately *may* be unbelief: "For I have nothing on my conscience, yet I am not thereby justified; but he who judges me is the Lord. Therefore, pass no judgment before the time, until the Lord comes, who will both bring to light the things hidden in darkness and make manifest the counsels of hearts; and then everyone will have his praise from God" (1 Cor. 4, 4-5).

The experience of free faith remains *before and for itself* essentially ambivalent; it is ultimately and inevitably endangered by the possibility of unbelief. This experience is in the last analysis the expression of that dreadful situation, namely, that the very ground of our existence down to its deepest level, our faith, is honeycombed with the hovering ambivalence of our freedom.[9] The experience of faith can never successfully and finally be disengaged from the abyss of unbelief.

This "existential overhang" of the believer's faith toward unbelief is left mostly in the background of the Catholic concept of

---

[9] K. Rahner, "Der Glaube des Priesters heute," in *Orientierung* No. 19/20 (1962).

faith because faith is seen here primarily as an *assensus intellec-tualis* to the unquestioned, because divinely guaranteed, content of faith. Nevertheless, the act of faith is called "at the same time" a free act: *simul est actus voluntatis* in the language of the *mag-isterium*.[10] Although we cannot here discuss more fully the prob-lem of this *simul* we want to point out that this qualification does not make the intellectual assent only indirectly free, in other words, the believer is not merely free when he freely establishes or admits the conditions under which he makes a mere intellectual assent, which is not formally free in itself. This assent must be described as *free in itself;* otherwise the act of faith *as such* would not possess dignity and rank as the highest freedom of man. Now, if the assent of faith must be called free in itself, then it is itself drawn into the existential danger of which we have been speaking. In other words, the believer can never know by himself whether his *assensus intellectualis* to the truths of faith is the true, per-sonal conviction of faith or only an opinion by which the doc-trines of faith are theoretically accepted and affirmed but have not yet become an existential structure of his affirming subjec-tivity. In short, the believer does not know whether he truly be-lieves *ex corde* or whether he only appears to believe *in facie.* The self-understanding of the believing subject is in an extreme degree irremovable from unbelief.

At this point, we could add to the discussion of the first phase of the implication of unbelief in the believer another determina-tion of the act of faith as given in the classical *analysis fidei, i.e.,* the description of faith as an essentially obscure act. This deter-mination, however, refers all too exclusively to the content of the act of faith, namely, to the supernatural mysteries which are the object of this faith. Apart from the problematic contained in the qualification of mystery as a truth which is withheld or not shown in its full light,[11] this determination of the act of faith has too

[10] Denz. 1791, 1814.
[11] Cf. for a criticism of this concept, H. de Lubac, *Discovery of God* (New York, 1960); K. Rahner, "Über den Begriff des Geheimnisses in der katholischen Theologie" (On the concept of mystery in Catholic theology), in *Schriften zur Theologie* IV (Einsiedeln, 1960), pp. 51-99.

little regard for its fundamental precariousness, its ever-present liability to be lost or to vanish, its self-concealment in the pilgrim believer.

We pass over this quality and mention in conclusion briefly and incidentally another characteristic of the act of faith: its lack of vivid concreteness (*Unanschaulichkeit*), *i.e.*, its *transcendence*. This quality of the act of faith which is taken seriously and unwaveringly by "negative theology" is of urgent actuality today. The infinite difference between the mental images and concepts formed from experience in this world on the one hand, and the truths of faith described in terms of those concepts, has never been seen more clearly than today. Never was the straight prolongation of experience and concepts gained from this world into an experience of faith more questionable than today. It is seen more clearly than ever that every similarity between the conceptual formulations of our faith and the faith itself which is so presented, is dominated, questioned and veiled by that ever greater dissimilarity;[12] or, as scholastic theology teaches, we can never with the univocal concepts of this world adequately grasp and express the realities of the faith.

Finally, the experience of the present-day secularization of the world,[13] caused by and communicated to us by the historical impulses of the Christian faith itself, has given us a heightened sense of the impossibility of visualizing the things of faith and their super-categoriality.[14] All world-derived concepts and proposi-

---

[12] We apply here the classical Axiom IV of the Lateran Council (cf. Denz. 432) to our question. It is evident from its dogmatic formulation that this axiom is to be considered not only and not primarily as a description of the ontic relationship between God and the world, but especially as a hermeneutic principle for the understanding of this relationship (*"notanda . . ."*).

[13] See the contributions of Balthasar and Rahner in this issue; also J. B. Metz, "A Believer's Look at the World," in *The Christian and the World* (*Readings in Theology*) (New York: P. J. Kenedy & Sons, 1965); *idem*, "Zukunft des Glaubens in einer hominisierten Welt" (The future of belief in a hominized world), in *Hochland* 56 (1964), pp. 377-91.

[14] "World" is here understood too much as "nature" or "environment" and not really as "companionate world" (*Mitwelt*) in the sense of the world of human interrelations, of which this sort of "secularization" can-

tional objectivations of our faith are also essentially concealing in character. This concealment of our experience of faith in its own concepts, so much recognized today, makes us realize again to what extent belief and unbelief interpenetrate each other in our conceptional consciousness; how much both may be hidden, before and for us, the one in the other; how little in us belief and unbelief are concretely separated from each other.

What has been said so far must suffice as an explanation of the first phase of the implication of unbelief in the believer. All of this explanation would be misunderstood if one would consider the here indicated concealment of faith in unbelief and its extreme precariousness as a "mere logical" or "mere psychological" one, affecting indeed the experience of faith but not the faith itself, *i.e.*, as if it "only" concerned the subjectively experienced approach to the faith. Such an understanding would separate faith and the experience of faith into two completely objective entities, as if we were able *quoad nos* to keep the experience of our faith and the possession of our faith apart. The fact is that the reality of the faith is in every case absorbed into the consciousness of the believer's experience of the faith. The two are inseparably united (not one and the same thing) in the ontological unity of the believing subject which as spirit, freedom, transcendence cannot exist otherwise than in a relationship of intersubjectivity, *i.e.*, in a relationship to others and through this to itself. Hence, all determinations of the believer especially the highest one, namely, faith, must exist in the form of intersubjective relationship of the self.[15] In other words, the concealment and precariousness of the faith, which is reflected in our experience of

---

not be predicated quite so univocally. In fact, to the extent that the surrounding cosmic world of nature shows its character as a thing-object, as "material" for man, can the singular significance of the *Mitwelt* and interhuman relations for the categorical interpretation of the act of faith become visible.

[15] On the interpretation of belief in the sense of experience of belief, cf. especially Urs von Balthasar, *Herrlichkeit* I (Splendor) (Einsiedeln, 1961); also J. Mouroux, *The Christian Experience* (New York: Sheed & Ward, 1954).

the faith, is a genuinely *ontological* concealment and precariousness of our existence as believers.[16]

2. The second, and for our considerations, really decisive
phase of the implication of unbelief in the believer becomes visible through still more precise formulation of the *theological* character of the precariousness of the faith. Thus, I think, we are
justified in concluding that Catholic understanding of the faith
also admits a real immanence of unbelief in the believer, a true
existential simultaneity of the two, a *simul fidelis et infidelis*.

In confirmation of our thesis we should recall that this precariousness of the faith receives still another and more incisive determination and qualification from theology. This precariousness
appears as temptation, described in theology as concupiscence.
Concupiscence as a quality of the believer's existence and experience of his faith entails more than that purely metaphysical twi-
light and precariousness in which his existence, due to his freedom and to his inner creaturely pluralism, remains incomprehensible, withdrawn and essentially insecure. There is neither
room nor a need here for an exposition of the nature of concupiscence and its inner connection with original sin whereby it is a
sort of *"negative existential"*, an inherited and ever-new lack of
justice-in-grace (*Heillosigkeit*) and an element of unbelief, all
of which place our faith in jeopardy.[17] We are here interested primarily and merely in stating that there is such a threat in the form
of temptation according to theology. True, this temptation is not
immediately and chiefly to be understood as a temptation of belief

---

[16] Here the question may arise how this description of the radical threat
to existence in faith is compatible with the teaching of theology on faith,
i.e., that the act of faith is an act of the *total* man. Where is there room
for unbelief? Our answer is that this existential totality of the act of faith
cannot be comprehended with fullness and clarity. Because the *whole* of
man is involved, the possibility of objective certainty about this engagement vanishes. It is exactly on the plane of reflective consciousness and
theological discourse that the act of faith becomes endangered and un-
certain. This does not exclude "firmness" and "certainty" which are contained and experienced in the act, as long as these qualities are not understood apart from the very act itself.

[17] J. B. Metz, *Konkupiszenz, Handbuch theologischer Grundbegriffe* I
(Munich, 1962), pp. 843-51; B. Stoeckle, "Erbsündliche Begierlichkeit,"
in *Münchner Theol. Zeitschr.* 13 (1963), pp. 225-42.

into unbelief but as a general temptation to sin, so that specific temptation to unbelief is only a particular case of this general temptation. This is another example of the strange darkness in the theological status of the question about unbelief in theology. However this may be, the doctrine of concupiscence seems to make possible a more radical understanding of the question about unbelief in the believer, by which may be elucidated the actual implication of unbelief in the believer and his experience of faith; in other words, the existential dialectic and perichoresis of believing-unbelieving. How can this be done?

If theology is unwilling to call the temptation of belief to unbelief itself *unbelief,* in the true sense of the word, it runs the risk of not taking seriously enough the radical nature and absolute interiority of this temptation as witnessed to by Scripture and Tradition. Although it is true that temptation to unbelief is not the same as formal unbelief, it is nevertheless true that man in the concrete experience of his faith, in which his faith is present to itself, cannot clearly recognize this temptation as a state of pure temptation (*"reine Versuchtheit"*) and in this sense successfully keep it away from his possession of the faith, nor can he enjoy this seeming success as *certainty of faith.*[18] The believer *before and for himself* never knows whether the experienced temptation to unbelief is *only* temptation, or whether it is not the manifestation of actually ratified unbelief in the incomprehensible complexity of his being: whether it is *only* concupiscence or the precipitation of existentially ratified unbelief. In this sense St. Paul in his letter to the Romans emphatically calls temptation to sin, *epidumia,* itself sin.

The teaching of Trent which clarifies this Pauline text and declares that temptation as such is not in itself formally sin, does not contradict our statement.[19] For the Council of Trent in defining the nature of concupiscence *in itself* does not assert that this concupiscence seen from an existential point of view, *i.e.,* as a reality

[18] This thought appears in Karl Rahner's treatment of the theology of concupiscence. Cf. *Theological Investigations* I (New York, 1961), pp. 347-82.
[19] Denz. 792.

in us, in the framework of our concrete experience of faith and justification, can be experienced as a *mere temptation* and thus clearly be seen as *not-sin.* In our personal experience of temptation—this experience is not added later to the temptation but belongs to the very nature of *our* concupiscence—we cannot rise once again above its dialectic; in the mirror of our concupiscent experience of faith and justification (*Heil*), we meet ourselves always as just *and* unjust (heil *und* heillos), as spiritual *and* of the flesh (pneumatik *und* sarkisch), as believing *and* unbelieving. In *this* sense the experience of the inner threat to us through sin can and must be called real sin; and Catholic theology recognizes the *simul justus et peccator.*[20] In this sense the experience of the inner threat to our faith by unbelief (by what else?) can and must be called real unbelief; there is a Catholic understanding of *simul fidelis et infidelis.*

This immanence and existential simultaneity of unbelief in the believer must yet be clarified in two directions. First: correct and necessary as it is to speak of our personal experience of faith in the sense of *simul fidelis et infidelis,* so it would be wrong to attempt to see as identical (*durchschauen*) this existential *simul* (the experience of ourselves as believing-unbelieving) and the essential *simul* (all belief is at the same time unbelief), and thus to resolve them. For the dogma of the Church teaches us that faith as a gift of grace does not simply coincide with the structure of our experience of faith. The action of God in offering and granting the grace of faith has a deeper and more comprehensive reach into man than is its manifestation in the concrete intersubjective experience of belief.[21] Besides, such a turning of the existential *simul fidelis et infidelis* into a statement about the essence of faith and unbelief would not specify and sharpen the paradox of the concrete experience of faith but would weaken it and level it down. For the ambivalence and awesomeness of *our individual* experience of faith would be resolved into the *general* proposition

[20] Karl Rahner, *Gerecht und Sünder zugleich;* R. Kösters, "Luthers These 'Gerecht und Sünder zugleich'," in *Catholica* 18 (1964), pp. 48-77; 193-217.

[21] K. Rahner, *Gerecht und Sünder zugleich,* p. 437.

"belief is at the same time unbelief", and would thus lose its edge. This "essentialization" and the concomitant generalization of this dialectic, which the Council of Trent rejects, is eventually seen to be a mistaken attempt at depriving the experience of faith of its existential burden.

Second, according to what we have just said, we can and must speak of the *unbelief of the believer* but not of the *unbelief of belief*. Despite this restriction, however, the impression could arise that in this relationship of *believing-unbelieving*, the believer was drawn into a fatal existential contradiction. This impression is avoided or at least rendered less acute when we consider a characteristic of subjective belief which we have not yet mentioned explicitly, namely, its essential and irremovable *intersubjectivity*. What do we mean by this? It is the very simple, yet in theology, not very common understanding that the believing subject, according to biblical and Christian teaching, is not the individual "I" as such (*in seiner Jemeinigkeit*), but the "I" in its original and continuous intersubjectivity, in its *brotherliness*.

Omitting here some thoughts touching our subject, we may say that the belief of the individual is actuated by lovingly and trustfully resting in the belief of the others, of the community, of the "Church" and *her* "subjectivity". Thus it gets a footing in the true transsubjectivity of an always greater belief.[22] Of course, belief cannot settle down on this ground altogether uncritically and without commitment. This supporting ground must be gained ever and again by a loving opening of oneself to others, in a never finished battle against the other alternative of his existence, *i.e.*, refusal of the loving opening of oneself to one's brother and the community. For the significance of concupiscence in the act of faith applies in a very special manner to the intersubjective foundation of this act. For concupiscence appears always and emphatically as enmity to, and questioning of, this interpersonal

[22] K. Rahner, "Dogmatische Randbemerkungen zur Kirchenfrömmigkeit" (Dogmatic marginal notes on piety in the Church), in *Schriften zur Theologie* V (Einsiedeln, 1962), pp. 379-410.

relation in belief, *i.e.,* as an urge to "isolation" from the brother and the community. Thus there remains for the believer and the reflexive consciousness of his faith the correctly understood *simul* of believing-unbelieving which he must overcome continually for himself under the impulse of brotherly love.

Before concluding our discussion of the unbelief of the believer, we may be permitted a short *excursus* on the subject of the intersubjectivity of the act of faith. According to our position, one may call this intersubjectivity an essential if not *the* central determination of the Christian believer.[23] (Moreover, it seems to be crucial for any appraisal of all actualistic or existentialist approaches to the theology of faith.) For the basic fact from which Christian theology has to proceed in any determination of the process of believing as well as the relation to God in general, is not, formally speaking, a subject-object relation but a subject-subject relation: the "I-thou" relation of the accepted or refused brotherly love. However, the adherents of the trend known as theological personalism, who claim this insight as their own, have somewhat darkened and emptied the importance of this insight by speaking of two intersubjectivities: the anthropological or horizontal "I-thou" relation between men and a theological vertical one of the "I-God" relation.

Prescinding from the fact that the use of the intersubjectivity between man and man as a model for man's relation to God, this intersubjectivity between men is considerably generalized and made objective, thus dissolving the basic fact; prescinding also

[23] The very rudimentary development of this fundamental aspect in the theology of faith seems to be due to the generally too formalistic character of our tract *De actu fidei.* We find there first a schematic statement of the act of faith to which is subsequently added the doctrinal content. Hence, the so stated act of faith does not mirror the "inner form" of this content; it does not reflect the inner structure of the act in the believing subject. This can be illustrated with a number of examples. Where, *e.g.,* does this sort of analysis speak expressly of the eschatological structure of the act of faith? In this connection express mention would have to be made also of the fundamental intersubjectivity, the "brotherliness", the ecclesial character (in the widest sense) of the act of faith. It seems all the more imperative to overcome this formalistic approach to the act of faith, since today it is not individual doctrines of faith that are questioned but the very possibility of the act of faith as such.

from the fact that the direct transfer of the relation between men to the relationship with God cannot do justice to the singularity and incommensurable character of the divine Thou, we cannot but observe that this interpretation and use of intersubjectivity by the theological personalists hides or prevents two other essential insights. The first is that the one (and only) intersubjectivity between men is of itself open toward God; in biblical language: in brotherly love salvific love of God takes place, "passage from death to life"; or in the words of dogmatic theology: the love of neighbor itself is *virtus theologica*. The second insight is that the specifically Christian subject of man's relation to God is not the individual man in his singularity (soul-God) but as one with all men (*Mitmenschlichkeit*), in his brotherliness of the "I-thou". Only thus is he his own real self in the depth of his personality and existence. For what is most personal in man occurs not in the *privatissimum* of monadic subjectivity, but in love. But these remarks are meant only as an aside to the central fact of the act of faith.[24]

Moreover, we cannot here refer to the other basic structure of the act of faith, namely, *hope*. An exact consideration of hope would more successfully demonstrate how every kind of pure formalism and actualism in the description of the dialectic of the believer's faith can be avoided.

III

Our discussion of unbelief in the believer as we have discussed so far is not, as some may think, dangerous mysticism or intellectual toying with unbelief. Rather does it lay bare the question-

[24] Concerning the significance of this question, cf. Urs von Balthasar, *Glaubhaft ist nur Liebe* (Only love can be believed) (Einsiedeln, 1963). The philosophical development of intersubjectivity is as yet in its first stages. It arose first and took immediately an antitheological turn in the so-called "Hegelschen Linken" (the left-wing Hegelians), *i.e.*, with Feuerbach, Marx and Nietzsche. Philosophical personalism can be mentioned here only with qualifications, because it is rather a phenomenologically orientated existentialist philosophy which at the same time deals with the transcendental problematic of the understanding of human existence. As an example, cf. E. Levinas, *Totalité et Infini* (The Hague, 1961).

ableness of our existence in faith at any time, and it teaches us to repeat, not in mere imitation or false pretense, the biblical words: "I do believe; help my unbelief" (Mark 9, 23). This insight makes us realize with new urgency that we must work for our salvation "with fear and trembling" (Phil. 2, 12). It calls our attention pointedly to the fact that we are not the mighty and unconquerable ones, but God; that we are saved by considering our belief only in consideration of our brother and, through him, of God in whom the ultimate existential plurality and ambivalence of our believing existence is hidden again (Col. 3, 3). It gives us a better understanding of the fact that great believers who are saints of the Church, from St. Paul to St. Augustine and St. Theresa of Lisieux, have experienced and admitted this "overhang" of belief toward unbelief. Only where faith is thus willing to face unbelief does it come to realize that it is the very place where the absolute question about the meaning of concrete existence is asked, where nothing is *a priori* assured, clear and unquestioned.

This assessment of unbelief in the believer establishes the inner theological place and status of the question of unbelief, which is the object of our present search. Before this question becomes an apologetical question about the unbelief in others, it is anteriorly and more originally a question of the believer about his own belief. The believer considers the risk involved in his own belief. It is he himself and not the other that appears first as a possible unbeliever. At the same time the unbeliever who professes his unbelief in whatever way, is seen in a strange vicinity to the believer; he seems to occupy from the very start the same level of existential question as the believer. The unbeliever is not in the position of one who is disavowed prior to dialogue and argumentation. The believer, by his search for the belief of the unbeliever, questions his unbelief; he does not teach him as if with superior authority but is engaged in an earnest search for his own ability to believe. Only such an attitude, it seems to me, gives real credibility to our words addressed to men of no faith or of a different faith. This ardent option of the believer in favor of the

belief in the unbeliever does not play down the seriousness of
unbelief nor doubt the intellectual honesty of the unbeliever. It
is a quest of the believer for his own hidden faith which can
never be just one "standpoint" *at the side* of others in this world,
a standpoint which ideologically makes itself a universal and absolute by being intolerant to other standpoints.

IV

Now that the question about unbelief has been turned into a
question of belief itself, we must search anew for the implicit
belief of the unbeliever. One way would be, as theologians such
as Henri de Lubac and Karl Rahner have indicated, to see the
problem in the sense of a possible existential implication of faith
in the individual who reflexively understands and argues his position as that of an unbeliever. For it is possible for a reflexively
articulated explanation of one's position (*Existenz*) and the actual and immediate living out of this position (*unmittelbarer
Vollzug dieser Existenz*) to be two different things. This is the
more possible, the more immediate and existentially concerned
is the actual realization of this position. Indeed, Catholic teaching asserts the ever present possibility that a successful act of faith
is being supported by wrong theoretical arguments. Otherwise it
might be possible to conclude from correct theoretical interpretation to the correctness of the practice of faith (from *"Orthodoxie"*
to *"Orthopraxie"*); a procedure that would lead to a form of certainty about one's faith that is rejected by the Church.

Another task would be to investigate the possibility of the
theoretical implication of faith in unbelief, *i.e.*, a cautious attempt would have to be made to uncover the *theological* presuppositions in the prevailing forms of atheism today. Thus we
would begin to understand why atheism succeeds in a considerable degree to make extraordinary demands on men and to enlist
them for causes far beyond their own concerns.[25]

[25] Among others: H. de Lubac, *The Drama of Atheistic Humanism*
(New York: Meridian Press); Urs von Balthasar, *Die Gottesfrage des*

It would be well to consider whether and, if so, how modern atheists derive their direct or indirect assertion of the "unreality" of God through a heightened awareness of the increasingly prevailing experience of the world in its true and proper worldly character. This experience has its source and historical origin in the biblical and Christian faith which teaches that the cosmos and nature are not divine or numinous and therefore that God is not an element of the cosmos and nature (*kosmisch-naturhafte "Unweltlichkeit" Gottes*). Again we should try to discover the meaning given to methodological atheism by modern "scientific atheists" in the interpretation of nature. This methodology has really become possible and admissible through the Christian belief in creation and the incarnation, both of which declare the thing-character (*Sachlichkeit*) of the creature and its general purpose of service to man. This same belief shows forth the human interrelations as the point in the world which makes the world transparent and focusses it upon God.

We might also examine to what extent modern eschatological atheism with its claim that "the beyond is burnt out", indirectly and implicitly imitates that transposition of an a-historical concept of the beyond into a historically engaged concern about the future, which is ultimately rooted in the biblical experience of God and the world.

Finally, we might endeavor to see whether and how humanistic atheism of "pure brotherliness" seeks and invokes that numinous depth of human interrelations which has become manifest in the divine incarnation, with the result that all immediate relationship to God is mediated and disclosed by the love of neighbor.

These and other theological implications of present-day versions of theoretical atheism should be elucidated and developed.

---

heutigen Menschen (The question of God and modern man) (Vienna, 1956); J. Lacroix, *Le sense de l'Athéisme moderne* (Paris, 1958); B. Welte, *Nietzsches Atheismus und das Christentum* (Darmstadt, 1958); M. Reding, *Der politische Atheismus* (Graz,[2] 1960); J. Y. Calvez, *La Pensée de Karl Marx* (Paris,[6] 1963); J. B. Metz, "Zukunft des Glaubens in einer hominisierten Welt," in *Hochland* 56 (1964), pp. 377-91; also Urs von Balthasar in the same issue.

Efforts in this direction are not a matter of intellectual sophistication or mere questioning of the theoretical presuppositions of unbelief. They are not underhanded attempts, through ways suspected of ideology, to retrieve by pure speculation positions lost in the course of the history of thought. They are only the expression of the ever new task of the believer to snatch his faith from its concealment in the abyss of unbelief.

We cannot discuss these problems here but must content ourselves with what little we may hope to have accomplished, namely, to throw some light on the question about the fundamental theological place of unbelief and thus offer measure and credibility to the problem of the possibility of "anonymous" and implicit faith on the part of the unbeliever. This theological angle does not seem to be without importance at a time when the Church reflects upon its task and self-understanding as "the Church in the Modern World".

Henri Bouillard, S.J./*Paris, France*

Human Experience as the Starting Point of Fundamental Theology

Among the questions that arise when we wish to define the object and the method of fundamental theology, there is one at least which cannot be avoided: by what right and in what degree can fundamental theology start from human experience, and ought it to do so?

Before outlining a direct answer to this question, it will be proper to define the concepts we will be dealing with and to indicate what their relations are to each other. What do we mean by *fundamental theology*, by *human experience,* and by *starting point?*

Fundamental Theology

Nominally, the term *fundamental theology* obviously means the theological exposition of the foundations of theology. But if we consider the academic tradition of the last four centuries, we will note that it designates simultaneously and puts in the same bracket two disciplines that are distinct in their object and their method: apologetics, or the rational justification of faith, and the treatise on the grounds of theology, or sources of theological knowledge. It is clear that these two studies are fundamental to theology, but they are so in different ways. The treatise on the grounds of theology demonstrates how Scripture, Tradition, and the magisterium witness to divine revelation, and, on this score, they are the sources and criteria of theology. This discipline is invested with a dogmatic character from the fact that it receives in faith what these witnesses have to say about their own function and their authority. It posits what the Christian message itself considers to be the *dogmatic* foundations of the *science* of faith. The role of apologetics is quite different. Its task is to give an exposition, in a form legitimate in the eyes of the unbeliever, of what the believer considers to be the *rational* foundations of the *decision* to believe. To sum up, on the one hand the intention is to establish in faith the science of faith; on the other, we wish to lay foundations in reason for the act of faith.

It may be desirable that a difference of this kind should be evident in our terminology. If it were agreed to adopt the phrase *Prolegomena to Dogma* to designate the study of theological sources, the term *fundamental theology* might be kept for what is often called apologetics. In any case, this is the convention which we will adopt here, since the study of theological sources does not enter—at least directly—into the realm of the question we have asked. Moreover, it will be clear that the term *fundamental theology* is more adequate than *apologetics* to designate what is implied by a study which aims at the rational justification of the act of faith.

It is a recognized fact that today apologetics has a bad public image. There are some who are tempted to do away with it and to replace it by a dogmatic exposition of the nature of revelation and of the Christian faith. This is quite understandable. In the course of the last century and at the beginning of this one, concern to justify and defend the faith too often led to the neglect of positive teaching on the content of the Christian message. Moreover, apologists were frequently misinformed about the intellectual capacity of those whom they wished to convince and on the nature of the theses they thought they were refuting. They presented too many inconsistent arguments which they had to abandon ten years later. As a result of one defeat after another, one withdrawal after another, apologetics has been weighed and found wanting.

Our duty today is not to give up the attempt, but to learn the lesson, to become more wary, more reasonable, more scientific. Certainly, fundamental theology must first elucidate what Christianity itself means by the term *revelation*. But this is not its whole work. In fact, it is the constant teaching of the Catholic Church that faith is a reasonable act and that this character should be made manifest. It is also true that no reason to believe dispenses us from believing; faith is a free act. But one does not commit oneself to it without a reason. Again, it is true that the transition from unbelief to faith cannot be made without the grace of the light of faith, *lumen fidei*. But for all that, it still has a rational structure. This must be brought out. It is absolutely necessary for us to know how to present a rational justification for our faith. It is necessary when we wish to approach the unbeliever and convey to him from the very start something that will mean something to him. It is necessary, too, in order to strengthen the Christian in his faith and to help him to take his position with respect to the surrounding atheism or the ambience of non-Christian religions. Finally, this kind of thinking will permit him to understand his faith better because it will mean a return to fundamentals.

But this reflection will only be what it should be if we become conscious of its proper nature. The question has often been raised whether or not it constitutes a science which is theological in the strict sense—that is, a function peculiar to theology—or an area of human knowledge which is preliminary to theology. Its intermediate character makes it possible to present arguments in favor of both positions. What is important is to note that the man who speaks is in a position of dialogue: as a believer, he is addressing himself to the unbeliever, whether real or virtual, with the desire to justify the act of faith. It is impossible for him not to speak in the light of what the Church professes: if he does otherwise he is justifying something other than the Christian faith. From this point of view, he is speaking as a theologian. But what he says must have a meaning and a rational validity in the eyes of the unbeliever. What he takes for granted with respect to himself, he cannot presuppose in the consciousness of his interlocutor. Therefore, he must speak in human language simply as a man, the language of a historian or of a philosopher, a coherent discourse which bears within itself its own rational justification. This human discourse, which rejects the possibility of introducing any statement of faith in the chain of its demonstration, may, on this score, be considered as distinct from theology. But it is also possible to hold, with a large segment of Catholic tradition, that it constitutes fundamental theology in the deepest sense of this term, since it is developed by the believer with a view to justifying the act of faith, an act which is at the beginning of all Christian theology.

To understand its function with greater accuracy, it is important to take into consideration the nature of what is called *unbelief*. This negative term in fact covers a number of positive attitudes. No one is a non-Christian for the sake of being a non-Christian, but he is so because he has another way of establishing his relations with God, with the world, and with himself. He is a follower of a positive religion: Islam, Hinduism, Buddhism, etc. Or, if a man is an atheist, he is so after a definite fashion of viewing the world and life: he is an Epicurean, a Stoic, an Existentialist, a Marxist. Every man wishes to realize what he considers to be the essence and the perfection of man. Now, Pope Paul VI has stated, with all the authority of the magisterium, in the encyclical *Ecclesiam suam*, that at the heart of non-Christian religions and at the basis of the efforts used by atheists to explain the nature of man, there are authentic spiritual and human values. We do not have to combat them; we should accept them and bring them to their fulfillment. It is in this spirit that the necessary dialogue between Christians and non-Christians must be carried on.

To accept the religious values of humanity, to accept the great manifestations of human thought, culture and civilization, to show that they are finite and that they are open-ended with respect to another world, to show how Christianity brings to man what they cannot give him but what he nevertheless needs: is this not the essential function of fundamental theology as we envisage it? Is this not the perspective in which to see what is commonly taught under the name of apologetics? Henceforth, will it not be possible to say that fundamental theology is essentially the dialogue of Christian faith with human experience in all its dimensions?

Human Experience

Before examining this relationship in detail, we must define what we mean by human experience. This term has so wide a meaning today that it is difficult to circumscribe it, and it varies almost inevitably according to the context.

First of all, what is experience, generally understood? It is possible to say that it is the most immediate consciousness of reality. By *reality* we must here understand everything that exists, not simply things, people, events, but also a way of looking at things, a movement of the will, an action, a thought. What characterizes experience is immediate contact: it is always something felt or lived. Therefore, it is opposed to speculation, to pure thought. But we should not forget that this distinction itself comes from, or is the result of abstraction. An abstraction that is legitimate and necessary, it is true, but we should be careful not to erect as so many independent realities the terms to which it is opposed. Experience and reason are not, in human knowledge, elements which can be isolated from each other. They are distinct, but not divided, aspects of one and the same knowledge. Experience is implicit reason; reason is experience understood and made explicit. Nothing is apprehended without being to some extent understood; every area of experience implies in itself a rational structure which thought can render explicit.

The areas of human experience are multiple and each one has its proper structure. Thus, we have scientific experience, aesthetic experience, social experience, moral experience, religious experience, etc. But what should we understand by *human* experience? Obviously, it is possible to use the term as a simple collective expression designating the sum total of many different experiences. But in general the term has the function of drawing attention to the relation which exists between these different experiences and man. In the case which here concerns us, *human experience* means the consciousness that man has of the relation that exists between his divers activities on the one hand and the global significance of his life on the other. It is the experience of his life in its totality and in its meaning. If it is true that all experience is at one and the same time immediate contact and implicit reason, we must say that the rational structure implicit in human experience is nothing else but the logic of human existence.

If we wish to place human experience at the starting point of fundamental theology, clearly it will be necessary for us to disentangle this logic, to express it methodically and completely, to give a rational and coherent exposition of it. It is tantamount to proposing a philosophical anthropology. The task is a difficult one, and certainly one is ordinarily dispensed from it in pastoral situations. Some very simple remarks on an experience which it has been painful to live through are often enough to touch a soul. But we are not here dealing with the ordinary run of pastoral duties; we are talking about elaborating a fundamental theology, that is, a coherent discourse which will have universal bearing. If, with this end in view, we wish to begin with human experience, we must consider it in its totality and explicate its internal logic.

In this totality, we can include religious experience itself if we address ourselves to men who profess a religion. On the contrary, we will be abstracting from it if we consider those who call themselves atheists or agnostics. For reasons of simplification, I will be considering only this second case, the most ordinary one in the West.

The Starting Point

Having explained what we mean by *fundamental theology* and by *human experience,* it remains now to make definite the meaning of the term *starting point* in the question we are examining. The starting point of a journey is the place in which we get ready for the journey, but it is a place which we *leave,* in order to go elsewhere. Should we understand the term in this sense? Yes and no.

Fundamental theology, in the sense in which we understand the term here, should be couched in terms which are valid in principle for every mind, even for the unbeliever's mind. If it appeals to human experience, it is the human experience common to every man, not Christian experience. But it proposes to offer to the unbeliever reasons for believing in Christianity, reasons for seeking the experience of faith. Therefore, it invites him to go beyond common experience. And it does so in two ways. On the one hand, it presents the signs of revelation. On the other, it warns him that faith cannot be simply the concluding step in the exposition, that faith is a free commitment in response to the call of divine grace. If, therefore, human experience is the starting point for fundamental theology, its terminus must be the experience of God in the signs of his revelation. From this point of view, the experience common to all men is (ultimately) left behind.

But it must be said immediately that we do not absolutely abandon it. Its study should not be considered simply as a kind of "initial apologetics", preparing the subject to receive apologetics properly so-called. On the contrary, we must remain in permanent reference to it, from one end of fundamental theology to the other. For this theology will not perform its function perfectly if it does not define the conditions of "symbiosis" (co-existence) which obtain between Christian faith and human experience. Christianity does not ask us to neglect human values; it should consecrate them.

These reflections, which conclude our efforts to define the terms of the question, already indicate the answer which we must now formulate and justify.

II

Should fundamental theology begin in human experience? We must answer in the affirmative, and we must do so for at least two reasons:

1. The reference to human experience conditions the contact with the signs of revelation.

2. It conditions the interpretation of the Christian message.

The Signs of Revelation

We will analyze first the contact with, or the grasp of, the signs of revelation. Christian preaching and Christian apologetic have, from the beginning, made the most of the sanctity of Jesus, the excellence of his teaching, his miracles, the accomplishment of the messianic prophecies, as so many motives of credibility. Later on, they insisted also on the notes of the Church: holiness, catholicity, etc. What is the reaction of the men of our own day when we present them with these reasons to believe? Even among non-Christians, even among atheists, there are few who do not admire the life and teachings of Jesus, but they do not see in them the signs of a divine mission. For them, Christ is a great moral and religious genius, but he is not the Word of God. There is more argument about the notes of the Church. Many, even among Christians, are less sensible of her catholicity than they are of the small number of believers at the heart of the immensity of the human race; less sensible of her holiness than of her human weaknesses. As for the argument from prophecy, we know today how difficult it is to convey its exact meaning and its bearing. We are aware also of the reserve that greets the account of the miracles. The development of science and skill, the understanding of different religions, historical criticism—these have largely diffused skepticism where they are concerned. It is a fact that, for many Christians, the miraculous, far from constituting a motive for faith, actually creates a difficulty.

It is evident that to such minds the miracles reported in the Gospel must be presented in conjunction with other signs, in conjunction with the ensemble of the Gospel message and the life of Jesus. But the question which concerns us here is more fundamental. How can we help our contemporaries to discern a divine revelation behind the sum total of its signs? We do not forget that recognition of revelation supposes at once the illumination of the Holy Spirit and conversion of the heart. But we know, too, that this recognition is a reasonable act, *rationabile obsequium,* because it implies a perception, a discernment of credibility. And here we wish to understand why and how the referral to human experience conditions this discernment.

The reason is that God's revelation would have no meaning for us if it were not at the same time the revelation of the meaning of our own existence. For the signs of revelation to be understood for what they are, the subject must grasp that there is an intrinsic relationship between the mystery which they are said to manifest and our own existence. The subject must at least glimpse what the Christian faith contributes to the fulfillment of his destiny. No apologetic will touch him if it does not in some way achieve this. Miracles and/or other signs will leave him in his blindness if he does not understand that the Christian phenomenon to which they belong provides an answer to the question of our existence.

Now how can he understand this unless by discovering in human existence an opening, a summons, toward something which goes beyond all that man can, by his own activity, effect in the world? He must seem to himself to be in need of the salvation which would be given to him. Then the signs of a supernatural gift and of a divine revelation will take on all their meaning in his eyes.

It is not necessary, we may note, that the understanding of this "openness" to the beyond in human affairs should precede, chronologically, the understanding or knowledge of Christianity. Normally, the Christian message will help a man to become conscious of this openness and to define its significance. But it is important that he should grasp the correspondence between the internal logic of Christianity and the logic of human existence.

What we are advancing here is nothing new. Christian tradition has frequently appealed to the harmonies which exist between nature and grace, faith and reason. We may recall just one passage in the Constitution *de fide catholica* of Vatican Council I (Chapter IV, "De fide et ratione"): "Reason, enlightened by faith . . . can, with God's help, acquire a certain knowledge of the mysteries . . . by reason of their connection with man's last end." If it is true that the questions of God's existence and of salvation are present, at least obscurely, to all men, it is normal to hope that certain of them at least, with God's help, will be able to glimpse that connection, when it is shown them by the reflection of believers.

Interpretation of the Christian Message

Having said why the recourse to human experience conditions the grasp of the signs of revelation, we must now show why and how it conditions the interpretation of the Christian message.

In his work *Finitude et culpabilité* (II, pp. 326-7), the French philosopher Paul Ricoeur writes: "From every point of view we are children of the critical habit . . . It is impossible for us to believe without interpreting." These words would serve to characterize the inspiration of several theological works whose success is sufficient witness to the fact that they correspond to the preoccupations of many minds. We are thinking in particular of the work of Rudolf Bultmann, of Paul Tillich, and of that famous little book of John A. T. Robinson, *Honest to God*. Reading such works, the Catholic theologian realizes with anxiety and grief that the Christian message has been singularly impoverished in their pages. But he cannot fail to recognize that a question has been asked which is troubling many believers, a question which, henceforth, it will be impossible to evade.

A Catholic will avoid saying that the language of the Bible, in particular the language of the New Testament, is mythological. For the word *myth,* even with its value restored by the historians of religion, still keeps a pejorative sense, and it is inadequate. But we must recognize that biblical language is bound up with forms of thought, with a system of representations, which are not directly those of modern man. The language of the New Testament owes something to Jewish apocalypticism, to rabbinical thought, to Hellenic noetics. We cannot appropriate this language to ourselves without interpreting it. We cannot have it admitted without explaining it.

Moreover, this is the occasion to remind ourselves that when it is a question of God and his action, all language, ancient and modern, is necessarily *analogical*. This means that the affirmations of the Scriptures, and the terms of the preaching which interprets them, do not describe God as he is in himself, nor his action insofar as it is his. They describe them in relation to us, that is to say, by reason of our relations to God and his action, under the forms of these relations. St. Thomas has stated: "We do not know what God is, but what he is not, and what is the relation of all things to him" (*C. G.,* I, 30). He has made it clear that this is also true with regard to revelation: The latter, he tells us, does not make us know what God is; it makes us know him inasmuch as he manifests himself in his effects (*Sum. Theol.,* Ia, q. 12, a. 13, ad 1). There is a curious resemblance between this proposition and the one which occurs as a kind of *leit-motif* in the works of Bultmann: we cannot say what God is in himself, but only what he does in us and for us. The Thomist doctrine of analogy would permit us to take for our own use what is valid in the program of Bultmann and the other theologians whom we have named above. Catholic theologians, and Catholic preachers even more frequently, seem to forget this teaching. We comment on Scripture without reminding ourselves that the *res significata* cannot be arrived at except by a negation of the *modus significandi*. We speak of divine things as if they were human things. The result is that, in the eyes of outsiders or of educated Christians, certain of our expositions seem mythological.

We are also in our turn children of the critical habit. But the Thomist principle of analogy offers us a support and a guide at the moment when we take up again this word: we can only believe by interpreting.

In order to interpret the Christian message, we must, obviously, envisage it from the point of view of its having a meaning for all men, that is, insofar as it gives an answer to the question of the meaning of human existence. We must, therefore, confront it with the internal logic of human experience. This confrontation should not have as its result the reduction of Christianity to a system of truths immanent in human nature. It must safeguard the transcendence and the gratuitous character of the divine action, which reveals, ennobles, and redeems. To succeed in this, we must show that human existence is open to a gratuitous intervention of God in human history. On the other hand, we must always remain faithful to the exact tenor and complete meaning of the Christian message. At the cost of this effort, the interpreter will discover in it simultaneously the understanding of himself and the possibility of believing that here God has spoken.

The task which we have outlined is today one of the most important ones to be performed by fundamental theology. We must not hide from ourselves its difficulty. Nor should we misconceive the risk which the individual runs of impoverishing or altering the Gospel message. We know that the authentic interpretation of the message does not come from isolated individuals, but from the Church, and that the Church has her expression in the voice of the magisterium. But the magisterium itself appeals to the work of theologians. In the encyclical already mentioned, Pope Paul VI invites them to undertake this task. Those theologians who have the courage to do so, in spite of the difficulties to be met with and the risks to be run, have the right to expect from their colleagues kindly assistance and a criticism devoid of unjustified suspicion.

III

If fundamental theology must set out from a base in human experience, in the sense in which we have explained it, it will be proper, in this perspective, to throw into relief the logic of human existence. In other words, it will be fitting to recall the great outline of a philosophical anthropology. This can be conceived in several ways. We cannot either describe or discuss them here. I wish only to draw attention to two points, two exigencies which must be respected.

First, it is important not to speak solely of the negative aspects of human existence: failure, sin, suffering, death. Certainly, it is through their experience that we become conscious of our limitations, our insufficiency, our radical dependence, our need of salvation. It is, therefore, indispensable to consider them if we wish to make man attentive to Christianity, to open him to the faith. But let us beware of considering only them. We would then run the risk of presenting Christianity simply as a remedy for failure, some kind of a stopgap, and not as the principle of life which it should be. When we analyze human experience with a view to a fundamental theology, we must bring out the positive aspects as well as the negative: therefore, love, work, social relations, scientific research, artistic creativity, etc. Christian truth must be seen to appear at the end of each of these avenues.

In the second place, it is important to envisage human existence not solely under its individual aspect, but in its social and historical dimensions. Man is a historical being in this sense, that he realizes himself by choices elicited in time. But he is so even more correctly in the sense that he realizes his potential within a collective human history. It is precisely this which makes it possible to understand that divine revelation, instead of being made individually to each human mind, has taken place in history, and in a specific history. It is there that we can find the answer to Lessing's famous objection to the idea of a contingent revelation.

The suggestions which we have just formulated, and others besides which have been the object of this article, are very summary, it must be admitted.[1] They simply outline some of the exigencies which must be satisfied by fundamental theology.

[1] The reader will find fuller development in our book *Logique de la Foi* (Collection "Théologie," n. 60, Paris, Aubier, 1964).

Maurice Nédoncelle/ *Strasbourg, France*

Philosophy, Handmaid of Theology?

Before touching on the theoretical problem of the relationship between theology and philosophy,[1] it is good to recall that these sciences are man-made, and that men are possessed of varying temperaments.

We might even say that theologians and philosophers belong to two different races. If it were not for the danger of being irreverent, I would gladly compare them to cats and dogs who live under the same roof, but regard one another without affection. The philosopher—meaning here the Christian philosopher—is afraid of the theologian. He thinks that the latter is often guilty of snap judgments, that he makes grand affirmations, and facile connections, under the pretext that divine revelation serves as a guarantee, between hypotheses that are neither certain nor verifiable. The philosopher always wants to arrest the winged flight of the theologian; to say to him, "Not so fast; do not confuse the line of argument as you so frequently do . . ." But what the philosopher fears most of all is that the theologian will not hesitate to force him to make incursions into his field, and that he will use philosophy for the benefit of his own *Schwarmerei*, enthusiasms. Accus-

[1] The sole purpose of these observations is to open a debate. They are, in part, the result of a conversation with my two colleagues, MM. Plagnieux and Chavasse, whom I wish to thank here, while assuming full responsibility for the opinions expressed in the article.

tomed as he is to go along step-by-step, he is mistrustful of anyone who seems to know everything, and who walks among the mysteries as if he had been party to the councils of the Eternal Father.

For his part, the theologian is not any happier with the philosopher's approach. Recently, a friend of mine who knows my propensity for philosophical works, and who is himself a real theologian, sent me his latest book with an acknowledgment which gave evidence of characteristic timidity. He wrote, "The theologian trembles before the philosopher." These words seem to me worth thinking about. Why this fear?

First of all, the theologian feels that he is in the presence of someone who, as the saying goes, splits hairs, and submits the product of his reasoning to a pitiless critique. He quickly feels paralyzed by the intervention of the philosopher. Then, he registers the fact that this would not happen if the two fields had nothing in common. The fields and the language, too. Basis and form intersect. It is precisely in this middle ground that the theologian runs the risk of being ill at ease: his freedom is under observation. Finally, the theologian fears in the philosopher, even in the Christian philosopher, the virtual presence of a lay critic and an unbeliever. He is under the impression that the philosopher, who "does not believe" in the role of grace *as a philosopher,* only pays it lip service as a man; he suspects him of being one of the false brethren, always ready to sabotage his neat doctrinal arrangements, in spite of every possible protestation of good will.

This introduction, which I am afraid is a little long, was necessary in order to "situate" the problem concretely. It is difficult, even chimerical, to omit consideration of this diversity of characteristics, when we scrutinize the demands the theologian can make of the philosopher, and the response that the philosopher will make to his colleague.

I

Since I have to speak here of the demands of the theologian, let us come immediately to the best-known and the most controversial question. Does theology need philosophy as her handmaid, yes or no? According to the old axiom attributed to Peter Damien, the unhesitating answer must be *yes!* However, the medieval authors whom he has in mind put philosophy at the service of faith, rather than of theology, and the shade of meaning here should not be overlooked. Their conception of philosophy or of dialectic must also be recast: it is certainly not ours, nor is it strictly uniform.

The term *ancilla* is not very clear, and it can designate a whole range of quite different services. Is philosophy a *slave?* a *maid-of-all-work?* a *housekeeper?* or the *wife* in a more or less morganatic marriage? How many ways are there of *"coming-to-the-aid-of"?* How many different ways there are of being an auxiliary to theology! And even if it is a question of marriage, the status of a married woman is also a variable!

It has become fashionable today to recognize that philosophy has a real autonomy. We are a long way from the rather conventional style that is found, for example, in the *Confessio Philosophi* of Leibniz, where the theologian is reputed to say to the philosopher: "Laudo modestiam tuam; instrumentum in te habebo." [2] However, very recently a thesis at the Sorbonne, written by M. Tresmontant, is in certain respects not very far from resurrecting this way of speaking.[3] The author believes that all religion implies a metaphysical *Einstellung,* or attitude—what he terms a "metaphysical gesture". Hinduism requires an immanentist metaphysics, while Judaism and/or Christianity simply cannot be brought into line with such a teaching. What I still have not grasped in the very fine book of M. Tresmontant is the exact place of this profound metaphysic: does it agree with religion, and nothing more? Is it its preliminary basis? or its expression? or a little of all this at the same time? Whatever it may be, Christians in the course of history would have made their choice among available schools of philosophy, in line with the radical orientation prescribed by their religion. Little by little, a specifically Christian

[2] G. W. Leibniz, *Confessio Philosophi.* Text, translation, and notes by Y. Belaval (Paris, 1961), p. 110.

[3] Cf. Tresmontant, *La métaphysique du christianisme et la naissance de la philosophie chrétienne* (Paris, 1961).

philosophy was formed, in opposition to non-Christian thinkers. On this score, some questions remain to be asked: Did Christians arbitrarily choose certain of the theses presented to them by pagan thought, and reject others? Or did they really innovate, did they create original ideas? The examples given by the author are especially those which concern a choice between a Creator and a Demiurge, or between a soul which forms part of the divine substance, and a soul which is not so mingled, etc.

In the second interpretation, namely that of a radical novelty in the philosophical concepts proposed by Christians, philosophy would be very dependent on faith. Nevertheless, if one were to grant, like Gilson and like Tresmontant with him, that the philosopher should think on his own, one might argue that extreme dependence would not in any way hinder, but would rather promote autonomy. It would be as if faith, having whispered the answer in the philosopher's ear, the philosopher went on to discover by his own methods the demonstration without which there would be no philosophy. But isn't the theologian also autonomous in this sense? Must not every intellectual development be a personal reflection on what is "given"? The data can be of various kinds, but the method is always either hypothetical-deductive or hypothetical-connective. It receives the data and puts them into operation.

To describe what takes place, I will not say, therefore, that on the one side there is autonomy and on the other there is not. Rather I would say: the theologian asks the philosopher to ply his trade and to speak up, but he asks him to speak after he, the theologian, has spoken. The theologian encourages the philosopher to be positive and effective. Philosophy is somewhat like his child; a living child of whom he can be proud, because this child, this daughter, will be respectful and grateful. *Laudo modestiam tuam; instrumentum in te habebo.* . . . A living instrument, this must be insisted upon; a glorious offspring, capable of walking by herself, and on the right path.

This is a consoling vision of things, and consequently, it is seductive; perhaps, even, it is inseparable from the Christian outlook. Let is be noted, however, that Leibniz's phrase is indeed subtle, and that theology does not always ask philosophy to speak up. Sometimes, rather, it asks her to keep quiet, to make an admission of indigence and even of uncertainty, to question and not to be questioned. Such is, perhaps, the conception of Blondel, who seems at first to present philosophic certitude, and then, little by little, cuts the ground away from under his feet. He questions, if not exactly what he began by stating, at least what he must end by exploring. If philosophy wishes to go all the way under its own steam, it ends both in apotheosis and in failure; it is inevitably condemned to posit on its own the problem of the supernatural and not be able to solve it. It is a philosophy of insufficiency, at least in the vertical sense.

Certain theologians—probably Protestant ones—would go still further; they require reason to be their enemy. Karl Barth demands that philosophy (at least religious philosophy) be erroneous, and he cannot do anything without this beloved enemy whose flattery seems to him a perfidy. He does not want a handmaid, and above all he does not intend to marry the handmaid; he files suit for divorce before the wedding ceremony takes place!

But in all these attitudes, seemingly contradictory, what always characterizes the theologian is that he determines with prophetic assurance what philosophy has to say and to do. He insists that she will be either for him or against him; he predicts how she will act and he judges this action. *Instrumentum in te habebo.* . . . The formula is more difficult to get rid of than one would imagine. There is not much difference *in this respect* between the partisans of the direct power of theology and those of its indirect power, nor between our Catholic manuals and the *Dogmatik* of Karl Barth. *Resting-place* or *taking-off point,* philosophy is an indispensable subordinate.

The stranglehold of the theologian on philosophy is accentuated by pedagogy. For the teaching of theology demands the preliminary adoption of a widely accepted language and logic. P. Mesnard has shown—following, in this, certain German authors —how Luther was obliged to re-introduce philosophical teachings into the German universities, and that this movement, which began with a return to formal logic, ended by a return to ontology. With all the more reason then, does the Catholic tradition call for an underlying philosophy. Our professors of theology need students who have been trained in scholastic philosophy:

1. Because a uniform vocabulary is needed, an audience that will understand what one intends to say, *e.g.*, they must know the meaning of *essence, substance, cause.* . . .

2. Because dogma must be based on firm convictions, *e.g.*, the fact that there is a God, a soul, etc., must be established.

The theologian, it is true, does not wish his students to be philosophers except within certain limits; for if they go beyond the propaedeutic, there is the risk that they will no longer be well disposed toward a theological calling. A little philosophy leads to theology; too much of it can interfere with the recruitment of theologians, who undergo a vocational crisis all the more marked in that within their own discipline they experience the brilliance of, and are challenged by, the competion offered by kerygma, liturgy, etc.

The pedagogical demand is a worthy one. If we could put ourselves once and for all into the ways of the 13th century, all would be well. Besides, as professors we always have a nostalgia for this kind of thing. But in the measure in which history has given birth to different ways of thinking, the whole situation becomes problematic. So much so, that theologians are obliged to oscillate between two attitudes. On the one hand, they cherish their scholastic foundations. These are essential to their vision of themselves as teachers. On the other hand, in spite of the confusion in philosophy which is the result of differences in culture developed through the centuries, they are interested in these attempts; they know that they find in them indispensable occasions for renewal; they need them for research. This free and new philosophy is not their *handmaid,* but their *sister.* She is not always well behaved; but if they do not take an interest in her, they run the risk of paralysis. They no longer dictate to her; they try to learn from contact with her, and, above all, to understand her.

II

This second attitude leads me to the second part of my argument. The theologian—not perhaps the professor, but the seeker—turns to philosophy as to a spectacle; he wants to read in it spiritual adventures different from his own, adventures that can teach him things he does not even suspect. Perhaps in reflecting on this material he will understand revelation better. His mental attitude is not different from the one he adopts toward exegetes and historians. Thus, he is brought to practice reflection in many different fields. Ricoeur, apropos of Nabert, [4] spoke recently of this phenomenon; its fecundity is derived precisely from the fact that it is not connected with a source or a principle in absolute isolation.

1. *Anthropology* is the first field in which interest or concern is manifested. Let us take some examples. If we are satisfied to describe death as a separation of body and soul, then the theology of the cross will remain for us paltry and dry. If, on the contrary, we attempt to gather and deepen human experience on this subject, as have, for example, in different senses, Landsberg, Karl Rahner, and Mouroux, then we inevitably throw an appreciable light on the meaning of the redemption. Meditation on the death of man, whatever this death and whoever this man may be, is a stimulus to meditation on the death of Christ, and can renew its meaning. All the more reason for this when the man is a Socrates and the death, the death of Socrates. And still greater reason if, over and above the exact experience which is being described, is added a reflection on the experience. [5]

Likewise, who will deny that a deeper knowledge of mother-

---

[4] E. Nabert, *Eléments pour une éthique*. Preface by P. Ricoeur. (Paris, 1962), p. 9.

[5] It goes without saying that every caution must be used in facing the risks inherent in a given situation or experience, which I have used here just as an example, and which, by definition, is a presentiment, or a perception of another, not of a passage already realized by us, since we are still alive.

hood will contribute to a better theological grasp of certain aspects of Mariology?

The *gnôthi sauton* implied in a philosophical program not only throws light on the humanity of Christ or the humanity of Mary; it renders even greater services; it throws light on the being and the work of the incarnate Word. Thus, a deeper search for the meaning of human solidarity cannot but have repercussions on our exploration of the mystery of the incarnation. The Council of Quiersy in the 9th century declared: "Almighty God wishes that all men, without exception, be saved, although not all may be saved. . . . Just as there is, was or will be no man whose nature Christ Jesus, our Lord, did not assume, so there is, was or will be no man for whom he has not suffered" (Denz. 318, 319).

Is it not evident that it will be an advantage for us to know how relationships are established between human beings in the so-called natural order, and that if we do understand them, we will understand better the conciliar statements we have just cited? For certain ones of the Fathers, *humanitas* was then *quasi unus homo*. Their background was perhaps neo-Platonic; they were probably disputing the subject of traducianism. Are their ideas valid for us, or not? Do they better express what we think of human intersubjectivity? The answer cannot be indifferent to those who wish to determine the relation of human beings to Christ and the effects of the work of the redemption on the salvation of men.

In the same manner, the whole treatise on the sacraments is an offshoot of anthropology. It is so, first of all in general, for a concept of *the spiritual act* and of *the sign* is inherent in the meaning of the sacrament. The Scholastics, arguing about this in terms of matter and form, have sometimes ignored, or consigned to second place, the *intentio,* about which the Council of Trent is, however, more concerned. Would not the *intentio* be the very soul of the sacrament, insofar as it has a *sign-character,* that which binds matter and form together? Philosophers would have to say so. Intellect, which takes hold of the materiality of the sign, transforms it. It does so not only by the reflexive consciousness of intentionality, or by an associative pursuit of objective symbols, but by an aptitude for discovering the transparency of the data in relation to a transcendence that operates in them and in us. A purely associative theory of signs—such as we find in our manuals —enables us to penetrate the nature of the sacrament in a far less satisfying way than does a theory of efficacy-through-transparence, which, by starting from the notion of *intentio,* is alone capable of giving new meaning to the notions of sacramental structure and of *ex opere operato.* And what is indeed instructive here is reflection on the co-existence, or influence, at the level of philosophic anthropology.

If we now study the sacraments in particular, the same facts are borne out. Is it not significant that the history of religions focuses the largest number of rites of access to the divinity on sacred meals and sexual union? The meaning of this union seems to have more importance in this respect than what Pradines called the "sense of distance". In Christianity, these perspectives are not forgotten but are purified. The eucharist is indeed a sacred banquet. It is a sacrificial eating (manducation). Rooting it thus in the history of religions is not the essential thing, but it is bound up with the essential thing. Theologians have nothing to be afraid of here. St. John Chrysostom was not afraid of this fact: he prefaced his theology of the eucharist by a philosophy of repasts. And Bossuet strenuously insisted on the destruction of the species in the holy sacrifice. In addition, we again find the anthropological connection of death and of Calvary in this nucleus of Catholic teaching on the eucharist.

It would be easy to point out examples that pertain to the other sacraments. Thus it is not surprising that the supernatural understanding of marriage is aided by a philosophical meditation on love. Many modern thinkers have spared no efforts to show this. And it is not always in vain. In certain pages of Madinier, there are remarks on this theme which could never be found in the writings of St. Augustine.

But without further delay, let us come to a general conclusion. There is a philosophical teaching (both from a phenomenological and a metaphysical point of view) which is confused with an anthropology, and which is not a simple introduction to a theology of revelation, but which finds a place within it a sort of "predestined" part of it. In this respect, the supernatural is, purely and simply, nature elevated. The Schools say that the supernatural is an accident and not a substance in us. This way of speaking is sometimes equivocal, but it seems here to be very much to the point. Who could have any objection to this status of anthropology *within* theology, this integration to an order of new relationships by a kind of simple transposition? The justification for it lies in the fact that Christ is man. The human element can be immediately adapted to a theological perspective by the fact that the humanity of Christ is not an illusion, but more really human than our own because it is more perfectly human than ours.

2. There is a second philosophical realm whose implication would be equally fruitful for theology. This is the supreme metaphysical realm, that of *the investigation of being,* of the problem of God. Again we find ourselves faced with an immense program of research. Let us limit ourselves to a single point. Is not the Thomistic proof of God's existence a definitive proof, much more than a deduction or an induction, a kind of reduction? The lamented M. Rabeau saw this very well. *Anankè stênai.* . . . The abstracting mind is the term. There is an ontological dynamism of the mind, a deficiency of the world which is compensated for by the plenitude implicit in *mind.* Undoubtedly, this is what leads us to God himself, and what establishes his existence. This is the God of the philosophers. But is this Absolute incomplete *because* it is philosophical? Let us admit at least that it can be kept in its totality, and ennobled by revelation. Philosophy's mode of survival in the theological order does not differ essentially from what it was just now when we were speaking of anthropology.

3. However, there is a third region of theology where cooperation with philosophy is manifested in an entirely different way. I wish to speak here of theology as it was understood by the Fathers, of *the trinitarian life of God.* When the theologian treats of the place of the Word in the Trinity, are we not thrust beyond all borrowing and all analogy, even that of proportionality? Cer-

tainly, insofar as the theology of the incarnate Word offers us taking-off points within our human nature, just so far does the theology of the Word in heaven abruptly draw us far away from every
region inhabited by creatures. We can no longer foresee anything.
Our powers fail.

Nevertheless, perhaps this is true only in appearance. In any
conversation with theologians, three tendencies can be observed.
Some show themselves to be anti-psychological and even anti-
philosophical in their trinitarian speculations. Unfortunately,
they never cease to speculate, but they do so in a code, on data
whose trans-rational nakedness they preserve. For them, trinitarian
theology divorces understanding and explanation or explicitation.

But side by side with this tendency there is a second one. For
this second type of theologian, the human intellect left to its own
powers is able to find phenomenological and metaphysical indications which are capable of bringing about a better understanding
of the data of faith. Gregory of Nazianzen said of the Son that he
was from the Father, and that he was like the Father. Could these
theses be unrelated to human sonship and human fatherhood?
What is from below can serve for understanding what is from
above.

And finally, there is a third group of theologians. For them, all
theology must submit to a twofold and inevitable movement. On
the one hand, our natural experience and reflection imply a supernatural apprehension; or, to put it more precisely, our concrete
nature finds within itself the steppingstones which Blondel described, and which are related not only to the supernatural life in
us, but to the inner life of God. Thus, it is useful for the theologian
to listen to this witness. On the other hand, this movement would
come to nought if our trans-natural reflection did not make us
aware of the sacrificial offering which we ought to make of our
nature and of our philosophy itself. Even more, it would not be
anything at all unless a movement were produced by which light
and strength descend through grace into our faculties, and if they
were not the bearers of a revealed datum of the supernatural order which is the object of theological meditation.

Is not this third kind of theology the best? Not only is it useless to make an absolute separation between *theology* and *oikomonia* in the sense in which the Fathers use this term; but even taking the term of *theology* in its widest and most modern meaning, it cannot be isolated from philosophy, to which it is bound by a reciprocal osmosis, in use and even in specification.

But there are limits to this interpenetration or osmosis. The theologian has a much more interpellative attitude than the philosopher has. He thinks, so to speak, in the vocative case; he inclines to prayer; in any event, he thinks in the current of historical perception; revelation is *event,* and the dominant *event is the coming of Christ.* But philosophy is not concerned with proper names, and it takes a slanted view of events. It only examines ideas, and abstracts them from facts and/or persons, even when it is study-identified, will not always relish each other, and will often have ing the ideas that radiate from persons and the history of those ideas. This is the reason why the two specialists will never become difficulty in coming to a mutual understanding, although they will never cease to have the need of mutual consultation.

PART II

BIBLIOGRAPHICAL
SURVEY

Heinz Robert Schlette/*Saarbrücken, W. Germany*

The Problem of Ideology and Christian Belief

The term "ideology" is being used ever more frequently and uncritically. We find it in political, sociological, historical, philosophical as well as theological writings and in other scientific literature on religion. There are such expressions as natural law ideology, "Europa" ideology, ideologies of political parties, mission ideology, ideology of the future, bourgeoisie ideology and so on. Often the word ideology has a pejorative accent. In many cases it is but a (somewhat questionable) equivalent for the untranslatable word "Weltanschauung". In ordinary conversational language, which does not clearly define its terms, "ideological" often has the meaning of intellectual, theoretical, doctrinaire, with the implication that some point of obvious interest is made to appear as a learned theory, or a trifling matter is represented as an important matter of principle. These latter uses hint at the scientific and philosophical problems involved.

A considerable literature exists, not all of the same caliber, on the notion and "nature" of ideology.[1] In accordance with the purpose of this survey we shall consider those publications which inform us about the concept of ideology and its variations, and es-

---

[1] Cf. the bibliography in *Ideologie-Ideologiekritik und Wissenssoziologie*, ed. with introduction by K. Lenk (Neuwied, 1961), pp. 323-38, (Soziologische Texte 4).

pecially the present-day problem of ideology. Since hardly anything explicit has been written about the relation between ideology and religious belief, we shall analyze the relevant works in view of the purpose of our study. This will necessarily entail a certain onesided and incomplete presentation. This limitation, besides our restriction to the more important works in the German language, has however the advantage of immediately coming to grips with the central questions: Is religious belief, or is the Christian faith an ideology in any legitimate sense? What consequences follow from the use of this terminology and from what standpoint is it possible? Is it necessary or superfluous to protest against this classification of religious belief? What is to be said about (non-Christian) ideologies from the standpoint of Christian theology? No doubt the clarification of these questions will aid the self-understanding of religious belief and the very necessary discussion of the relation of the Church to the modern world. Since a survey of this kind cannot accomplish an exhaustive investigation or solution of these problems, its aim will be to explain only the problems involved and their present state.

The title of this survey purposely avoids the term *concept* of ideology because no commonly accepted *concept* exists. It has been shown that the modern idea of ideology may be variously modified due to its history. In fact it has undergone several metamorphoses. H. Barth has traced the important changes in the meaning of ideology on the basis of a great amount of historical material. [2] He begins with Antoine Destutt de Tracy who, following Locke and especially Condillac, develops in his "Les éléments d'Idéologie" (Paris, 1801-1807, 5 vols.) a philosophy that rejects all idealism and apriorism and seeks to explain the origin of ideas solely on the basis of sensation and empirical experiences. Barth remarks: "The *Idéologie* aimed to be an analysis of the human mind without regard to religious ideas that might contribute to the image of man. Despite this avowed hostility to metaphysics and

---

[2] H. Barth, *Wahrheit und Ideologie* (Zurich, 1945). Cf. also the articles "Ideologien" (H. Maus) and "Ideologie" (N. Birnbaum) in *Die Religion in Geschichte und Gegenwart,* Vol. III (Tübingen,[3] 1956), pp. 566-72.

the claim of providing an understanding of man derived exclusively from empirical sciences, Destutt de Tracy's 'Science des idées' retained all the basic ideas of the Enlightenment. These called forth the sharpest opposition on the part of the restoration's philosophy and doctrine of the State." [3] Understandably, Napoleon who considered atheism as the "principe destructeur de toute l'organisation sociale" [4] also considered the "Ideologists" as his natural enemies and attacked and ridiculed them as "obscure metaphysicians". Since then the term ideology denoting radical thought, which is not interested in practical realities but claims to represent "reality", has been ridiculed and despised by men of practical politics: it has become an invective.

Barth shows next how Bacon's theory of the "idols" in his *Novum Organum*, intended as a critique of reason which was to free the mind from all "prejudices", influenced Helvetius and Holbach. [5] These latter already recognized that ideas depended on the social environment and they began to "reveal" and "unmask" the power of the rulers as being based on "prejudices". These thoughts were most welcome to Marx as an illustration of Hegel's philosophy of the State and of history. Marx also knew Destutt's book and the meaning of the word ideology stemming from Napoleon. Yet, Marx gives this word a new perspective by bringing it in connection with the general relation between thought (consciousness) and Being, or, as Engels called it, a "false consciousness", *i.e.*, consciousness that necessarily results from a wrong socio-economic substructure (the "basis"). With Destutt, ideology was yet the positive description of a definite philosophy, which of course according to the men of practical

---

[3] *Ibid.*, pp. 30f.

[4] *Ibid.*, p. 29. On the other hand, the first ideology-critic may have been the ancient sophist Critias who declared that "belief in the gods was the invention of a wise statesman who wished to prevent people from doing wrong even in secret, by giving them the belief in all-seeing and all-hearing observers whom he placed in heaven." Cf. F. Ueberweg and K. Prächter, *Die Philosophie des Altertums* (Berlin,[12] 1923), p. 128.

[5] A positive interpretation of prejudice is offered by H.-G. Gadamer, *Wahrheit und Methode, Grundzüge einer philosophischen Hermeneutik* (Tübingen, 1960), pp. 255-75.

affairs and politics deserved nothing but ridicule. Marx makes ideology—not without some influence of Feuerbach's change from theology to anthropology—a term denoting all philosophy (more exactly of the "superstructure"). Of course, the "true" insights of Marx and his followers were excluded. Barth, how-ever, shows that Marx's aesthetics contains elements incompatible with his theory of ideology, since he teaches that art is not subject to the general condition of the substructure.[6]

Marx does not consider his views as an ideology but as the true knowledge of reality; his is "true consciousness" because it cor-responds with the reality underlying it. His concept of reality (*Seinsbegriff*) is, of course, already restricted by his own theo-ries. Here it becomes clear that the problem of ideology raises questions as to reality, being, knowledge, and answers them in a very definite way. Hence Barth is right when, after discussing Nietzsche's theory of ideology[7] and how it differed from that of Marx, he states: "Everything depends on how one conceives the nature of the human mind." [8]

But the meaning of ideology changes not only from Destutt de Tracy to Marx and Nietzsche. In recent sociology there has arisen a new notion that qualifies every non-empirical or, as some say, experimentally not verifiable, theory or statement as ideolog-ical, whereas the older view accepted only one, *i.e.*, the "true" way of thought and philosophy as not ideological. Hence, the new view considers any interpretation of reality that cannot be demonstrated in a strict scientific manner as an ideology. This concept of ideology has been developed especially in the pro-grammatic work *Ideologie und Utopie* by K. Mannheim,[9] which has made an extraordinary impression. Its methodology is con-sistent and its argument supported with philosophical reflections. Mannheim intends to prove that all thinking is a necessary re-

---

[6] Cf. H. Barth, *op. cit.*, p. 144f.

[7] *Ibid.*, pp. 207-82.

[8] *Ibid.*, p. 286.

[9] The book appeared first in Leipzig in 1929 and, after Mannheim's emigration, in London in 1937, and a third enlarged edition in Frankfurt in 1952.

flection of reality ("Seinsgebundenheit") and to this end he develops a sociology of knowledge. He is concerned with the control of the collective subconscious of man and with the discovery of a categorical possibility of "false consciousness". His concept of "total ideology" questions the whole epistemology of consciousness, *i.e.,* there is offered a critique of the classical ontology and metaphysics in favor of a "relationism" based on social and vital conditions. Thus the concept of ideology is enlarged and the basic model devised by Marx is incorporated in the sociology of knowledge[10] by Mannheim's assertion of the correspondence of reality and knowledge primarily as a reflection of social and vital conditions.

It is strange that Mannheim does not hesitate to speak of "Seinsgebundenheit"; he seems to think that he presents something new, whereas it is just another instance of the analysis, criticism and unmasking of "thought" common among the proponents of the sociological theory of knowledge. New, however, is his interpretation of reality and reality-correspondence (apart from its formal and material similarity to Marx's ideas). But this interpretation does not stand up under philosophical reflection since he arbitrarily restricts reality to the sphere of socio-economic and vital factors, subject to control and manipulation. No ancient or medieval philosopher would be opposed to "Seinsgebundenheit" of thought. But when we consider that at the "end" of Western philosophy, "being" means only the facts of sociology and vitality, we realize how much of true reality has been forgotten.

Much more radical and simplistic is the concept of ideology formulated by Th. Geiger,[11] who takes a neo-Kantian and logistic concept of reality as his norm. Whatever does not fit this dogmatically fixed scheme is called a value-judgment and consigned to the sphere of ideology where things can be neither proved nor

[10] Cf. Cl. Lefort, "Ideologienanalyse in der heutigen Gesellschaft," in *Ideologie-Ideologiekritik und Wissenssoziologie,* ed. K. Lenk, *op. cit.,* pp. 283-88.

[11] Th. Geiger, *Ideologie und Wahrheit. Eine soziologische Kritik des Denkens* (Stuttgart, 1953).

disproved but stand like erratic blocks in the field of reality and of human life in particular. Geiger does not hesitate to give as an example of an ideological value-judgment the proposition: The odor of the hyacinth is sweet,[12] since reality ("is") is being attributed to a subjective sensation. It is clear, according to the sociological epistemology and positivism of men like Marx, Mannheim and Geiger, that not only religion, philosophy, morality, jurisprudence are to be classified as ideologies; this includes, of course, Christianity as a special instance of religion. Geiger says: "Religious feeling evidently is no ideology since it states no proposition. . . . Dogmatic theology however is ideology and nothing else. It has not the least shred of reality. Its pronouncements and whatever is said about the objects of the pronouncements, are mere figments of the mind. The natural fear of the primitive has nothing to do with ideology. The figure of Pan bleating in the bush may be but a projection of this fear. But the serious assertion that there is such a being as Pan is sheer ideology. The frightened person has transposed his feeling of fright into a proposition asserting the existence of a reality, according to which the object of his fright is supposed to have bodily existence." [13] Similarly the proposition "God is almighty" is said to be "for the mind completely meaningless" and hence an ideology.[14]

If it were a question of a mere label we might not object too much to calling Christianity an ideology especially since the distinction between science and ideology is sometimes said to involve no prejudice as to their respective values. But Geiger also denies in principle the truth-character of the Christian tenets and considers them as beyond the pale of rational reflection. Religions,[15] being nothing but ideologies, are mere functions of vitality-relations[16] or according to V. Pareto rationalizations (De-

[12] Ibid., pp. 54-56.

[13] Ibid., pp. 75f.

[14] Ibid., p. 76.

[15] Cf. Religionssoziologie, ed. F. Fürstenberg (Neuwied, 1964) (Soziologische Texte 19).

[16] Cf. Th. Geiger, op. cit., p. 68.

rivate) of affectivity-relations (*Residuen*)[17] which are automatically disposed of as the substructure changes. Geiger has made the widest application of the notion of "false consciousness", meaning by it the objectivation of subjective value-judgments, *i.e.*, subjective experiences of the will and sentiment. Here is used a scientific conception[18] that corresponds to Comte's law of the three stages. In fact, Comte must be considered as one of the fathers of the modern concept of ideology even though he himself spoke a different language.[19] M. Bense's idea that as a result of scientific progress the problem of religion and of Christianity was being solved automatically follows the same line,[20] *i.e.*, positivism. His thought has the same formal structure as that of Marx and Lenin and he hopes for the same effect although for different reasons.

The preceding survey shows that the contours of the concept of ideology are fluid and that the discussion of the problem of ideology is more important and helpful than the futile attempt at a neat definition. J. Barion published a small work entitled *Was ist Ideologie?* [21] intended as an inventory. The merit of the book consists exactly in offering a brief yet clear and comprehensive survey not elsewhere available, but it contributes nothing to the clarification of the problem. Toward the end of his book Barion says: "Ideologies are closed systems, they admit no rational criticism, they know only the error of *all others*. Ideology demands unqualified acceptance (*Bekenntnis*); science is the progressive effort at obtaining knowledge. Ideology and science are radically

[17] Pareto's main work, *Traité de sociologie générale,* appeared in Lausanne and Paris, 1917-1919, 2 Vols.

[18] Cf. G. Söhngen, "Positivismus," in *Lex. Theol. Kirche,*[2] 1957, VIII p. 637f.; cf. also W. Stegmüller, *Metaphysik-Wissenschaft-Skepsis* (Frankfurt, 1954).

[19] Cf. A. Comte, *Rede über den Geist des Positivismus,* translated with introduction and commentary by I. Fetscher (Hamburg, 1956) (Meiners Philosophische Bibliothek, Vol. 244, with bibliography).

[20] Cf. M. Bense, "Warum man Atheist sein muss," in *Club Voltaire* I (*Jahrbuch für kritische Aufklärung,* ed. G. Szczesny, Munich, 1963), pp. 66-71 especially p. 71.

[21] *Studie zu Begriff und Problematik* (Bonn, 1964).

irreconcilable opposites." [22] Another view of the polarity of science and ideology is possible if one sees them indeed as opposed and not too antagonistic toward one another, but rather as complementary, perhaps in the way that Heidegger distinguishes science and reflection (*Besinnung*)[23] and Jaspers contrasts philosophy ("the truth") with the different branches of natural science.[24]

A more intensive study of the problem of ideology is made possible by K. Lenk's collection of texts.[25] After an introduction to the history of the problem Lenk offers well-chosen and systematically arranged texts from old and recent literature on the subject. In "The Critique of Mythology and Religion" there are texts from Bacon, de Jaucourt, Holbach, Feuerbach, Freud and Topitsch. The Marxist criticism of ideology and its further development are presented with passages from Marx, Lukács and Bloch. For the positivist view we have citations from Comte, Durkheim, Halbwachs, Pareto and Geiger; the "German sociology of knowledge" (according to Lenk) is represented by Scheler and Mannheim. The work concludes with criticisms of the sociological theory of knowledge by Tillich, H. Marcuse, Plessner, Horkheimer, Adorno, C. Wright Mills, C. Lefort, L. Kolakowski. We cannot possibly discuss these important and dense writings. Some objections could be raised; *e.g.*, it is hardly possible to circumscribe positivism as the author does. The work is, however, an excellent means for scientifically penetrating the whole complex of the relevant problems and is otherwise extremely helpful, especially since some of the texts presented are not easily available.

We turn now more directly to the question as to what the concrete issues of the problem of ideology are today; what tendencies and standpoints are of special interest with regard to the subject of our study. The main forms of ideology are still the Marxist, the

[22] *Ibid.*, p. 106.

[23] M. Heidegger, "Wissenschaft und Sesinnung," in *Vorträge und Aufsätze* (Pfullingen, 1954), pp. 45-70.

[24] Cf. K. Jaspers, "Wahrheit und Wissenschaft," in *Universitas* 16 (1961), pp. 913-29.

[25] Cf. footnote 1.

socio-epistemological and the positivist. Of these, the Marxist conception demands the clearest and most explicit description.

Here a return to the specifically Marxist concept of ideology must not be overlooked. Connected with this is a criticism of the self-understanding of the official Marxism-Leninism as an ideology and the endeavor to overcome ideology as much as possible through science. Robert Havemann, the East Berlin scientist and philosopher, clearly states the Marxist conception of ideology in his lectures published under the title "Dialektik ohne Dogma". He says: "What men think derives from the society in which they live. Part of this may be actual knowledge (*Einsicht*) or consciousness, but most of it is *ideology*. The ideas that society produces about itself in the minds of its members, ideas that have no scientific character but yet belong to this society as a condition for its existence: these are ideology. We know that Marx and Engels gleefully derided the ideology of the Germans. They have written *Die deutsche Ideologie,* in which they delightfully berate the tendency of the Germans to escape from the tearful vale of reality into the pale heaven of their ideology. Hence we really misuse the word when we speak of ideology in a positive sense; and the name "Ideologische Kommisson" for a committee whose function is the promotion of social consciousness is a *Contradictio in adjecto*.

"The purpose of the Communist movement is the very abolition of all ideology. Consciousness must take the place of ideology, *i.e.,* the self-deception corresponding to the state of society, Our aim is to spread scientific understanding about ourselves and our social situation." [26] Furthermore, Havemann distinguishes in the Marxist sense, between the "class consciousness" of the workers and their class ideology. This latter, he says, exists only among the workers in capitalist society and manifests itself as "Trade-Unionism", *i.e.,* as a "pure unionist type of thinking which is interested only in gaining economic benefits within the

[26] R. Havemann, *Dialektik ohne Dogma. Naturwissenschaft und Weltanschauung* (Hamburg, 1964), p. 110.

existing society. The aim of unions is not to revolutionize the world and to battle for throwing off of the chains." [27] Havemann also points out the relationship between ideology and morality saying that "morality is the most perfect way of concealing true social conditions." [28]

G. A. Wetter and W. Leonhard have published two very substantial and instructive volumes under the title *Sowietideologie heute*[29] concerning the present philosophical, economic and political doctrines of Marxism-Leninism. The word "ideology" in this title should not be taken as a "Western" or positivist term. Although Communist self-understanding considers historical and dialectical materialism as a "scientific world-view" the Communists have begun to use the term ideology officially in a somewhat un-Marxist and incorrect sense as a term to describe their own system. Thus the program of the 22nd Congress of the Communist Party in 1961 declares: "The modern world is the theater of a bitter struggle of two ideologies, the Communist and bourgeois." [30] Leonhard adds short comments to each chapter and in comparing the Soviet ideology with the Soviet "reality" discovers discrepancies. There can be no objection to this method. Yet reflection on the "reality" and the "facts" indicates the fundamental problem which is an eminently philosophical one, namely, what understanding of reality may be used as a basis? Leonhard seems to take an exclusively empirical position of fact-finding but not of strict positivism. This makes his comments all the more persuasive.

In this connection we want to mention also the position of the Warsaw philosopher L. Kolakowski.[31] He objects to the too un-

[27] *Ibid.*, pp. 111f.
[28] *Ibid.*, p. 117; cf. *ibid.*, pp. 117-27.
[29] Vol. 1: G. A. Wetter, *Dialektischer und historischer Materialismus* (Frankfurt, 1962); Vol. 2: W. Leonhard, *Die politischen Lehren* (Frankfurt, 1962).
[30] Quoted from *Perspektiven der sowietischen Politik. Der XXII. Parteitag und das neue Parteiprogramm. Eine Dokumentation*, ed C. W. Gasteyger (Cologne, 1962), p. 178.
[31] Published in German: *Der Mensch ohne Alternative. Von der Möglichkeit und Unmöglichkeit, Marxist zu sein* (Munich, 1960).

critical formulation of "scientific ideology" and "the camp-followers of the ideology which claims to be scientific". Kolakowski believes "that science will gradually emancipate itself from control by the ideology". This, however, does not mean that there ever will be art without "ideological inspiration". Kolakowski considers the call for the complete delivery from ideology a "naïve fiction". Thus he limits his position in two directions: "The hope for the rise of a scientific ideology . . . and again the hope for the drying up of ideology are unfounded".[32] Kolakowski's thoughts are courageous, well-founded and instructive for the theologian who learns how a convinced reform-Marxist views the Church and theology as an ideology.[33]

The main problem of non-Marxist philosophers and sociologists in discussing ideology seems to be the question about the significance which still attaches to present-day ideologies. Different answers are being given. Besides the general trend to overcome or restrict ideologies, there are those who point out the positive meaning of ideologies for human and political existence. These two positions need not be taken as opposites since both are interested in opening up or keeping open those areas of life that can be entered only by voluntary decision. In all this there is still a positivist element which is, however, considerably mitigated since the metaphysical standpoint taken rather resembles that of Kant and not that of the neo-Kantians.

There exists a brief yet clear survey of the present sociological interpretations of ideology by D. Rüschemeyer under the title *Mentalität und Ideologie*.[34] "Ideology and mentality differ in the first place by the degree of their reflexive penetration and formulation. *Mentalities* are relatively little clarified complexes of opinions and conceptions," *e.g.*, workers' mentality, village mentality. Ideologies generally are "more or less systematic formulations of mentalities". The distinction is made between ideologies that

[32] L. Kolakowski, *op. cit.*, p. 38; cf. *Ideologie und Theorie*, pp. 24-39.
[33] Cf. Especially the chapter "Der Priester und der Narr. Das theologische Erbe in der heutigen Philosophie," *op. cit.*, pp. 250-80.
[34] "Soziologie," in *Das Fischer Lexikon*, ed. R. König (Frankfurt, 1958), pp. 180-4.

"sanction the *status quo* and prevail among the ruling classes, and the ideologies of groups whose norms, aims and conduct differ." [35] These latter groups are usually more explicitly conscious of their ideology. Rüschemeyer points out that Mannheim's conception of total ideology has discredited the position of ideological criticism since the kind of relationship between "situation and outlook" (*Seinslage und Sicht*) asserted by him would render all knowledge relative. This is also the criticism leveled against him by C. A. Emge.[36] The reason given is that factual statements can be tested empirically and thus ideologies can be "unmasked" by the social sciences. Yet, it is admitted at the same time that "the criticism of value-judgments transcends the limits of science". Here, however, the concept of empirical knowledge is not quite clear and in need of logical analysis. At any rate it is gratifying to know that modern sociology, in principle, no longer questions the objectivity of values, but simply considers them not susceptible of scientific testing.

With this understanding present-day sociology prescinds from value-judgments in its research. It is certainly no accident that this conclusion of Rüschemeyer's article is found in a work published by René König and is thus worth reporting as indicative of the present situation of the problem: "More recent research, which is much less influenced by ideological discussions, tries to devise a more objective approach, namely, a non-valuing analysis (*wertfreie Betrachtung*) of value-charged clusters of ideas whose underlying conditions as well as their effects on the structure and changes of society are susceptible to investigation. This separation of ideology-research from ideological discussions advances slowly which explains the presence of some ideological elements. It also explains the frequent opposition to such non-valuing re-

---

[35] Cf. D. Rüschemeyer, *op. cit.*, pp. 181f.

[36] Cf. C. A. Emge, *Das Wesen der Ideologie, Ein Versuch zur Klärung in Hinsicht auf Antizipation, Perspektive, Vorurteil, Ressentiment, Selbstverständlichkeit, sich übernehmende Denkansprüche und dergleichen Vorwegnahmen mehr*, Mainzer Akademie der Wissenschaften und der Literatur, Geistes- u. sozialwissenschaftliche Klasse 1961, 1 (Wiesbaden, 1961), pp. 58f.

search or the suspicion that it is partisan in a hidden or at times unconscious way." [37]

This poses the crucial question whether "non-valuing investigation of value-charged ideas" is possible. It cannot be denied that it is possible, under rigorous observance of methodical self-limitation on the part of sociology. In fact, sociology, if it is not to become philosophy, must work without value-judgments. How else could it arrive at objective criteria? By adhering to this self-limitation sociological epistemology and positivism must forgo judgments of metaphysical and ethical truth. Research thus defined cannot judge whether "race-ideology" is right or wrong. At this point we must ask, however, whether this sort of self-limitation can have any meaningful results. Consistency no doubt demands this. We must also keep in mind that renouncing value-judgments cannot lead, *e.g.*, in the race question—as *mutatis mutandis* in all other questions—to race-ideology because no "valuing" at all is being done.

At this juncture non-valuing criticism of ideology has to make a choice. Either it remains tolerant toward all, admittedly unverifiable, "value-charged ideas" to which, of course, religion belongs, and suspends judgment on their truth and worth; or it will consider what cannot scientifically be verified as entirely irrelevant, subject to being unmasked and as a view to be destroyed through scientifically "critical enlightenment". On this point the opinions advanced in the ideology literature differ widely.

H. Kelsen and his school practice a very pointed criticism of ideology and are passionately interested in the unmasking of the ruling-class ideology and the various forms of social metaphysics supporting it. The collection of articles by Kelsen from the years 1923-1957 edited and introduced by E. Topitsch[38] contains important studies, from the standpoint of ideology-criticism, of the platonic conception of love, justice and the idea of the good as well as of Aristotle's political theories. Basically it is a critique

[37] D. Rüschemeyer, *op. cit.*, p. 184.
[38] Cf. H. Kelsen, *Aufsätze zur Ideologiekritik* (Neuwied, 1964) (Soziologische Texte 16).

of philosophy, or better, metaphysics on the part of sociology very much like that of Geiger. His discussions are of eminently actual importance for our own political concerns. He is right in pointing out that it is not the positivism of the Enlightenment, contrary to the prevailing notion, but the metaphysical ruling-class ideologies of the Western tradition that have some affinity with authoritarianism, as the events of 1933 in Germany showed. Deserving of our attention is Topitsch's reference to the so-called "empty formulas" of metaphysical thought such as *the* good, justice (*suum cuique*), the natural law, conscience, etc. These, he says, are so formal that they allow themselves to be filled with any content; in fact this void calls for ideological content that can always be made to serve the ruling classes.[39] These "nonvaluing" reflections of Kelsen and Topitsch are not free from polemics against the whole Western tradition; they set up the positivist concept of science as an absolute by which they judge all the historical value systems.

The same attitude characterizes E. Topitsch's highly informative and methodologically consistent article "Begriff und Funktion de Ideologie". In justice to him we must mention that Topitsch is here as in every other point more discriminating and cautious than Geiger and admits that "the value of any insight as such" depends on "a theoretically and scientifically unverifiable assumption". He declares, futhermore, that empirical sociology is "still far away from a complete understanding of the conditions underlying the truth of scientific statements about reality."[40] Yet, he is hopeful about the increasing "de-mythologizing, de-ideologizing, de-fanaticizing" results of science and "scientific enlightenment".[41] Thus he looks forward very real-

---

[39] Cf. E. Topitsch, in H. Kelsen, *op. cit.*, pp. 14-16; *idem*, "Begriff und Funktion der Ideologie," in *Sozialphilosophie zwischen Ideologie und Wissenschaft* (Neuwied, 1961), pp. 15-52, especially pp. 37-41 (Soziologische Texte 10); cf. also Topitsch, "Über Leerformeln. Zur Pragmatik des Sprachgebrauches in Philosophie und politischer Theorie," in *Probleme der Wissenschaftstheorie, Festschrift für V. Kraft*, ed. E. Topitsch (Vienna, 1900), pp. 233-58.

[40] *Idem*, "Begriff und Funktion der Ideologie," pp. 42f.

[41] *Ibid.*, pp. 50-2.

istically to the passing of dialectical materialism "only through the development of a modern post-Marxist science that takes place at an equal pace both in the East and the West".[42] It would have been welcome if Topitsch in this article had explicitly discussed the question whether he felt that some legitimate area (beyond scientific control) was possible, free for the unfolding of metaphysics and religion. In view of his criticism of metaphysics elsewhere[43] we may well ask whether the method of the "empirical social sciences" and "ideology criticism" has the required hermeneutical equipment; in other words, whether criticism of metaphysics is not rather a problem of philosophy and can be done better by it.[44]

C. A. Emge, although much less polemical than Geiger, Kelsen and Topitsch, has on the whole similar views at least as regards their general trend. He sees in ideologies "a synthesis of old-type, idealist systems and axioms".[45] According to Emge, ideologies have a tendency toward totality, they are "holistic" and are sometimes given concrete expression in "utopias".[46] Their power stems from the emotions, they radiate a charm, they make use of empty formulas. Although Emge deals specifically with "the opposite of ideology", his ideas on this point are not very clear. He seems to have in mind a limitation of man's mind and action to what is closest to him. He thinks that it is part of human nature to accept lacunas. He does in no way profess a positivist attitude but rather envisions a "new pragmatism" without specifying the suppositions and implications of such a position.[47]

---

[42] *Ibid.*, p. 50.

[43] *Idem, Vom Ursprung und Ende der Metaphysik. Eine Studie zur Weltanschauungskritik* (Vienna, 1958).

[44] H. Krings, "Ein Dialogfragment über das Ende der Metaphysik-soeben aufgefunden," in *Epimeleia. Die Sorge der Philosophie um den Menschen, Festschrift für Helmut Kuhn,* ed. F. Wiedmann (Munich, 1964), pp. 13-18; M. Müller, "Ende der Metaphysik?" in *Philosophisches Jahrbuch* 72 (1964), pp. 1-48.

[45] C. A. Emge, *op. cit.,* p. 42.

[46] In regard to this problem which we cannot examine here, cf. especially E. Bloch, *Das Prinzip der Hoffnung.* 2 Vols. (Frankfurt, 1959).

[47] Cf. C. A. Emge, *op. cit.,* p. 76.

The intention of overcoming the ideologies appears, much more clearly in W. Knuth,[48] than in the authors mentioned above. He does not pursue this objective in the manner of "science" or positivism or pragmatism, but by turning to "the original views of, and attitudes toward, the world". He considers ideologies as derivations from a reflexive world image. This contrast of "reflexive" and "immediate" must be called unsuspectingly innocent in view of the modern discussions about ideology and its most recent history.[49] Recourse to what is immediate is not capable of critical control and hence itself ideological. His characterization of National Socialism, Marxism and Communism as well as conservatism and what he takes to be "liberalism" is unconvincing. Thus, the book is disappointing because what it proposes is dangerous and illusionary; it is indeed "Gnosis" in Voegelin's sense of this word.[50] Knuth believes: "The complete conquest of the ideologies would be a life without ideologies, original and individual in its striving for self-realization, bound by the primordial images and values of community life and free in its absolute faith in transcendence."[51]

Marx already attacked the *Deutsche Ideologie;* an apparently new version of this ideology has been satirized by Th. W. Adorno with elegance of style and biting wit.[52] He declaims against the recent philosophy of existence (existentialism) and personalism (Heidegger, Jaspers, Bollnow and, according to Adorno, also Buber). He accuses these authors of substituting an aesthetically and philosophically insufferable jargon for argumentation. The irrational has overpowered reason, he claims, and the social basis of philosophy is not being respected. Adorno does not take up

[48] *Ideen, Ideale, Ideologien* (Hamburg, 1955).
[49] *Ibid.,* pp. 52f.
[50] On Voegelin's concept of Gnosis cf. E. Voegelin, *Die neue Wissenschaft der Politik. Eine Einführung* (Munich, 1959), pp. 153-259. It would be a rewarding work to compare this concept of Gnosis and Gnosticism with the problems of ideology.
[51] W. Knuth, *op. cit.* (The sentence is given emphasis by Knuth.)
[52] Th. W. Adorno, *Jargon der Eigentlichkeit. Zur deutschen Ideologie* (Frankfurt, 1964).

the social aspect of ideology[53] but offers in this polemical tract a noteworthy analysis, the intriguing feature of which is his own way of accommodating the concept of ideology. We need not enter upon the controversy of Adorno with Heidegger which predominates in this book.

For many, ideology is not a subject of scientific discussion but rather something to be put in brackets or to be destroyed. The way of science, the way to reality and to the practical concerns, promises delivery from ideologies. This view is opposed by E. Spranger[54] who believes that what is positive in the ideologies can be saved by considering them as "idea-schemes of the future". Hence, they make no pronouncements about the actual reality and cannot, therefore, be subjected to critical tests of truth. Here, use is made of a subjectively restricted concept of ideology which is scarcely distinguishable from utopia and planning for the future. Since all projections of the future are based on principles derived from the present and the past, such anticipations of the future must be subject to critical examination by reason. Geiger incidentally considers the idea of *progress* as a theoretically inadmissible objectivism of subjective wishful images, *i.e.,* ideologies against which we must be warned.[55]

A brief but illuminating summary of the theories about the role of ideologies in modern society is contained in the respective chapter of H. Freyer's book *Theorie des gegenwärtigen Zeitalters.*[56] He reflects especially the scientific pretensions of the ideologies themselves and comes to the conclusion: "Ideologies are deformed religion rather than deformed science." [57] With this thesis the old question about the concept of religion becomes again acute. Knuth also called the ideologies, frequently but in

[53] This is done in "Ideologie," a contribution to *Soziologische Exkurse* (Institut für Sozialforschung, Frankfurt, *Frankfurter Beiträge zur Soziologie,* Vol. 4 (Frankfurt, 1956).

[54] E. Spranger, "Wesen und Wert politischer Ideologien," in *Vierteljahrshefte für Zeitgeschichte* 2 (1954), pp. 118-36.

[55] Cf. Th. Geiger, *op. cit.,* pp. 86f.

[56] Stuttgart, 1955, pp. 117-32.

[57] H. Freyer, *op. cit.,* p. 127.

a rather confused way, substitute religions. The problem of ideology is moved, however, to a different plane when it is interpreted as a special case of religious behavior. One need not deny that ideologies absorb and activate religious energies, as Berdyaev and Monnerot have shown in the case of Communism.[58] Yet, modern criticism of ideology ordinarily considers religion as a special case of ideology.

An important book on the problem of ideology has been written by the Swiss philosopher, Mme. Jeanne Hersch.[59] It deals openly and directly with the current political ideologies. For Madame Hersch, ideologies do not coincide with the respective political parties. She is very careful and exact in her distinction of the political ideologies; she mentions the fascist, communist, liberal-conservative, progressive-democratic and the socialist types which she describes in detail. She calls this the geography of ideologies. We are here not concerned with this part of her book. Deserving of more attention is her dispassionate attitude toward the whole complex of questions, exemplified by her statement: "It is wrong and crude to assert that ideologies do not count, that they are all lies, and that only actions count. Ideologies themselves are actions and factors of reality." [60] Madame Hersch leaves aside the socio-epistemological and positivist criticism of ideology, but underlines the necessity and usefulness of having an ideology for one's personal, social and political life. Lack of interest in questions of ideology or in any ideological engagement leads, she says, to an emptiness of human life. Thus Madame Hersch in her book, written with passionate fervor from democratic-socialist conviction, points to an existentialist and anthropological need. The Communists can agree with her, but also the Christians who consider the *"colloquium salutis"*, to which the dialogue between the ideologies belongs, as meaningful, possible and necessary.

[58] Cf. N. Berdyaev, *Wahrheit und Lüge des Kommunismus* (Darmstadt, 1953); J. Monnerot, *Soziologie des Kommunismus* (Cologne, 1952), pp. 245-399.

[59] *Idéologies et réalité* (Paris, 1956).

[60] J. Hersch, *op. cit.,* p. 38.

The studies of Adorno, Spranger, Freyer and Hersch have brought about a certain expansion of the scope of the concept of ideology; this is due to the indeterminate use of the word ideology. The basic philosophical and social problem, however, is that which we presented in connection with our discussion of Mannheim, Barth, Emge, Geiger, Kelsen and Topitsch. A theological confrontation with the problem of ideology faces the necessity of distinction, choice and limitation, *i.e.*, the necessity of elaborating first of all the *status quaestionis*. The critical sifting of ideology-criticism is primarily the task of philosophy whose attitude is, needless to say, of great importance for the theologian.

From this point of view the keenly penetrating studies of H. Plessner demand special attention. Even though his works appeared for the first time in 1931 [61] and 1935 [62] they have lost none of their actuality nor of their cogency. Plessner shows the philosophical uncertainty in the starting point of the sociology of knowledge and especially in the positivist distinction between science and ideology, and thus deprives radical ideology-criticism of its self-assurance. Assertions that history is the "fundamental dimension of human life", that there is nothing in human knowledge and consciousness "which has not undergone a process of formation through subjective categories", but especially that "vitality" and "life" are the "substructure" and guiding force of every thought process: "these propositions", Plessner declares, "have to be decided by philosophy",[63] and ideology-criticism has been too hasty in considering them as clear and settled. Plessner also protests sharply against sociology's Marxist scheme of thought. "Sociologists and historians who make such general use of the idea of ideology just as if this notion were unpolemical or suprapolemical whereas in fact it was devised as a weapon, give the ominous impression that it was possible for the social sciences

---

[61] H. Plessner, "Abwandlungen des Ideologiegedankens," in *Zwischen Philosophie und Gesellschaft. Ausgewählte Abhandlungen und Vorträge* (Bern, 1953), pp. 218-40.

[62] *Idem, Die verspätete Nation. Über die politische Verführbarkeit bürgerlichen Geistes* (Stuttgart,[3] 1962).

[63] Cf. H. Plessner, *op. cit.*, pp. 238f.

to accept historical materialism and to believe at least in the superstructure conception of Marxism as in an eternal truth. It is time that this detachment of the concept of ideology from its original context of ideas and the change of its technical meaning for the sake of a rather loose use in empirical research be forcefully opposed. For neither research nor politics are interested in the false peace between sociology and Marxism, which has been brought about by the more or less deliberate change of the concept of ideology into a category of empirical sociology." [64]

And now the important question: What is the situation in regard to the theological literature on the problem of ideology? Theology and faith itself are very strongly challenged by ideology-criticism. Despite this fact, no real and direct confrontation of theology with the problem of ideology-criticism has taken place. We must add, however, that themes like "knowledge", "history", "action", "religious experience", "reality and worldliness" and others, do implicitly concern the problem of ideology. Hence it would be wrong to say that theology has up to now taken no cognizance of the sociology of knowledge and of Marxist and positivist ideological thought. Still we must note that an explicit theological answer to ideology-criticism is as yet lacking. There are a few studies which must be mentioned in our survey.

R. Hernegger has published the first volume of his 3-volume work entitled *Ideologie und Glaube. Eine christliche Ideologienkritik.*[65] The title does not, however, imply that Hernegger treats the problem in the sense of our exposition above. He proposes to develop an ecclesiastical self-criticism in which revealed truth or Sacred Scripture is the frame of reference within which must be determined what is ideology in the Church and as such must be overcome.[66] Hernegger uses the same terminology in his second

---

[64] *Op. cit.*, p. 239. We can do no more than point to the important chapters in Plessner's *Die verspätete Nation* (pp. 106-27) where he tries to show that both the supernatural authority of God and the natural authority of reason are completely discredited due to a general suspicion that their dictates are mere ideology.

[65] The title of the volume is *Volkskirche oder Kirche der Glaübigen?* (Nürnberg).

[66] Cf. R. Hernegger, *op. cit.*, pp. 12f.

volume[67] which deals with "the Christian ideology as a justification for power struggle in the Church". It must be admitted that Hernegger raises serious theological and pastoral problems, each of which demands careful examination. In regard to the problem of ideology that interests us here, he does not contribute anything, apart from his rather arbitrary transfer of the concept of ideology to the area of the Church. The concept of ideology can be applied to the inner life of the Church—by the Church to the Church—only with certain reservations. For in this case ideology in the sense of ideology-criticism is the "frame of reference", *i.e.,* Sacred Scripture and the faith, which Hernegger posits as extra-ideological. But this constitutes the very substance of Christianity and not mere historical developments in the historical and always peccable Church. Hernegger's critical observations could find better support on the basis of a phenomenology of religion, sociology and theology, if the dogmatic distinction—known to Hernegger—between *religion* and belief were upheld with greater consistency.[68]

Also a new collection of articles with the promising title *Christlicher Glaube und Ideologie*[69] will disappoint any reader who looks for a confrontation with ideology-criticism or the ideology problem. Only J. Ratzinger's contribution deals with the proposed theme.[70] Ratzinger, it seems, applies Mannheim's concept of "particular ideology" [71] to Catholic social doctrine and concludes that the doctrine of natural law which claims to be Christian is not free from "a good dose of conceptions that are condi-

---

[67] *Macht ohne Auftrag. Die Entstehung der Staats-und Volkskirche* (Olten-Freiburg/Br. 1963), pp. 17-21 and *passim.*

[68] Cf. H. R. Schlette, "Der Katholizismus als Religion," in *Deutscher Katholizismus nach 1945. Kirke-Gesellschaft-Geschichte,* ed. H. Maier (Munich, 1964), pp. 79-102.

[69] Ed. by K. Von Bismark and W. Dirks (Stuttgart-Mainz, 1964).

[70] Cf. J. Ratzinger, "Naturrecht, Evangelium, und Ideologie in der katholischen Soziallehre. Katholische Erwägungen zum Thema," in *Christlicher Glaube und Ideologie,* pp. 24-30.

[71] Cf. K. Mannheim, *Ideologie und Utopie,* p. 53: "We are dealing with a particular concept of ideology when the word is used to indicate that one is not prepared to believe certain definite 'ideas' and 'conceptions' of an opponent because they appear to be more or less conscious ways of hiding the true facts which the opponent does not want to be known."

tioned by the times". Since he considers this "as an element tenta-
tively designated as 'ideological' ",[72] he implicitly admits the possibility that there may appear and actually have appeared in the
Church such pronouncements as "according to natural law" and
"Christian" which cannot be proved to be such by natural law and
the Gospel. Hernegger repeatedly voices this thought and illus-
trates it with historical and theological examples. Justified and
necessary though these reflections are, they are no theological
answer to the problem of ideology-criticism as it is posed by
Mannheim, Geiger, Kelsen, Topitsch and others.

This problem is taken up explicitly for the first time by Karl
Rahner in his article "Das Christentum und der 'neue Mensch' ".[73]
The scope of his discussion is limited, however, to "Zukunftside-
ologien" (futurity-ideologies). Rahner sees the urgent necessity
of examining the concept of time held by these ideologies and
utopias. He points out the time-conditioned situation of the Christian personality and of the mind and of every personality in its
actual reality. With these factors as the foundation and point of
reference, is it possible for the futurity-ideologies to have any
meaning at all? "Only if there is a future for the personal, individual spirit," he says, "struggle for a better future of later generations will make sense." [74] In the light of theology the ideological schemes for the future are already "anticipated" (überholt)
because to the believer not only the meaning of history and the
destiny of man are revealed but still more because the Christian
by his faith experiences the future as something already accomplished.

We have tried to show the problem indicated by the title of
this survey by discussing a few selected publications. It is evident
that much is yet to be done by theology. If genuinely non-valuing
sociology considers it necessary to call faith an ideology, this is
in itself indifferent and no cause for protest. A very serious matter, however, is the radical distinction between science and ide-

[72] J. Ratzinger, op. cit., p. 27.
[73] In Schriften zur Theologie V (Einsiedeln, Zurich, Cologne, 1962),
pp. 159-79.
[74] K. Rahner, op. cit., p. 170.

ology. For this makes possible attacks on ideology by declaring it more or less openly as a self-deception and a means of deceiving others. In reality, the positivist type of ideology-criticism is all too smug in its pretensions and breaks down when subjected to philosophical examination. Even recent historicists begin to doubt its value. [75] Nevertheless, it still possesses the plausibility common to all popularizations and is welcomed by many as a comfortable defense against the disquieting questions of metaphysics and religion.

Ideology-criticism poses a number of open questions for theology. Does the freedom of the act of faith justify a contrast between science and the area of belief (or ideology, if you will)? What is the *experiential basis* of belief in the sense of Sacred Scripture, namely, the *history and historicism* of Christianity? Is positivism the result of a self-understanding of reality and the world, which by placing man in the center of a secular context of creatures, makes possible a specifically Christian way of human existence? [76] Does there exist such a phenomenon as "structural Christianization" or, better even though linguistically worse, "structural Hebrewization" of man's thought and attitude in an altogether formal sense and fully apart from personal assent to a definite religious "content"? What is the significance for philosophical and theological anthropology of the still existing possibility of the rise and continued existence of ideologies beside and outside of exact science? Has the singularity claimed for faith as opposed to non-Christian religions special consequences for the problem of ideology? Confrontation with the Marxist and Western sociological ideology-criticism will not be embarrassing to theology only if it has the courage to tackle its indeed massive objections. The necessary effort to study these problems will be the only way of advancing a step forward in the self-understanding of faith and belief.

[75] Cf. *e.g.*, E. Nolte, *Der Faschismus im seiner Epoche* (Munich, 1963), p. 56.

[76] Cf. J. B. Metz, *Christliche Anthropozentrik. Über die Denkform des Thomas von Aquin* (Munich, 1962), pp. 117-34; *idem*, "Weltverständnis im Glauben. Christliche Orientierung in der Weltlichkeit der Welt heute," in *Geist und Leben* 35 (1962), pp. 165-84.

PART III

DO-C DOCUMENTATION

CONCILIUM

DIRECTOR: Leo Alting von Geusau
Groningen, Netherlands

ASS'T DIRECTOR: M.-J. Le Guillou, O.P.
Boulogne-sur-Seine, France

Josephus F. Lescrauwaet, M.S.C./*Stein, Netherlands*

The Reformed Churches

About 25 percent of Christians today profess the Gospel and live their baptism according to the insights and in the spirit of the 16th-century Reformation. In number they are about 200 million, and they are distributed among 1,000 or 1,100 Churches,[1] according to one's method of classification. In trying to determine their place in Christianity throughout the world, one discovers at once two obvious factors: on the one hand they dissociate themselves from the Catholic, Orthodox and Old Catholic Churches, while on the other they are not in full communion with each other, either in belief or in practice. This might tempt us to put them all under the one collective heading of "Protestantism" or to draw up a catalogue of all the individual Reformed Churches or Church groups. In neither case would the Reformed Christians recognize their own situation. We know from our ecumenical experience that our partner in the dialogue never represents "Protestantism" in general and that this dialogue is not basically conducted with one of the thousand Reformed Churches, but rather with a representative type of Church. The

[1] Grundler, *Lexikon der christlichen Kirchen und Sekten,* Vols. I and II (Vienna, 1961).

distinctive types of Church which now exist within the Reformation may be reduced to a few.

The use of the notion "type of *Church*" requires further justification. For too long has the opinion been prevalent that the concept "Protestantism"—as opposed to "Orthodoxy" and "Catholicism"—confers only a negative unity on those who reject the historical Church. Such a Protestantism would be based in principle on a Churchless attitude in which actually existing Reformed Churches would use historical structures and means simply for practical purposes in order to support the faith of the individual.

Both Catholics and Reformed Churchmen used this idea of Protestantism currently during the last two centuries. Now, however, on both sides—first on the Protestant and consequently on the Catholic side—it is becoming ever more clearly realized that Reformed confessions of faith definitely bear witness to the Church, and that each Reformed community looks upon itself as a form and visible realization of the universal Church of Christ, that each considers the written Word of God, baptism, the Lord's supper and even perhaps other sacraments to be the foundation of the Church, and that their communities strive after that form of the Church which comes closest to that of the apostolic and sub-apostolic age.

The Lutheran professor, Peter Meinhold, maintains that every Reformed community "wants to be the catholic and apostolic Church in the true sense of the word; it does not merely want to assert the presence of Christ's Body in itself, but wishes to express this outwardly and thus claim to be the true, pure, holy, catholic and apostolic Church; for all Churches, therefore, the Church in her historical appearance is a central and essential part of their very belief—otherwise the outward appearance of the Church would not have been the object of the fiercest debates".[2]

The fact that we have to deal with Churches and ecclesial communities is, however, no reason to draw up a more or less complete catalogue of all separate Reformed Churches. For many of these

[2] P. Meinhold, *Ökumenische Kirchenkunde* (Stuttgart, 1962), pp. 274-5.

Churches have the same confession of faith and the same structure; they are only separated from each other from the administra-
tive point of view for secondary reasons such as country or
language, because of fortuitous historical processes or because
of accidental differences of theology or spirituality. The separate
organization of Reformed Churches is therefore less important
for an understanding of Reformed Christianity than the five or
six dominant types of Church to which many of these communities can be reduced.

We talk of a separate *type* of Church when (a) there is an
essential difference in the principles of *faith,* as, for example, the
Augsburg Confession of the Lutherans compared to the Geneva
Confession of the Calvinists; (b) and/or in the principles of
structure in the community ("Order", "Structure", "Verfassung"),
as, for example, the episcopal as distinguished from the presbyteral
order.

The boundaries are not always clear nor historically constant,
and the ecclesial awareness, which is growing in the great
Churches of the Reformation, blurs the theoretical distinctions.
In addition, even within one and the same Church are often to be
found still other lines of demarcation such as those between
orthodoxy and liberalism and between pro- and anti-catholicizing
tendencies. In general, however, those on the Reformed side will
recognize themselves in the following main types: Lutheran,
Calvinist or Presbyterian, Anglican, Free Church and the missionary and united Churches in mission lands. Next to this list is the
sect which in itself may not be called a type of "Church" but
which will be discussed here insofar as it has a reformed character.[3]

[3] W. van de Pol, *World Protestantism* (New York: Herder and Herder,
1964).

I

THE LUTHERAN CHURCHES

1. *The Name*

The 166 Churches that fall under this heading originated from Martin Luther's attempt at reforming the Catholic Church. Separated from this Church with his followers (juridically in 1520, existentially perhaps a decade later), he considered his own community of Christians as the true continuation of the one early Church of the New Testament, in which the Gospel was preached in its purity and the sacraments (baptism, the Lord's supper and confession), administered according to that Gospel. This is why many of these Churches call themselves "Evangelical" or "Evangelical-Lutheran" Churches.

2. *Confession of Faith*

Their faith concentrates on the Person and work of Jesus Christ as the central content of the Gospel which he preached. This view of the faith is given us in the Scriptures and is confirmed by the tradition of the early Church. Holy Scripture is the sole "source and norm of the faith", and as such it is the highest and ultimate authority for the Church's teaching and action. With this Scripture, there is room for ecclesiastical confessional writings that express the Church's witness according to the temporal circumstances in which the Church has to confess her faith. Lutheran Christians accept the various formularies of faith, brought together in the *Book of Concord* of 1580 and comprising the three ecumenical creeds, the Confession of Augsburg, the Apology for the Confession, the Articles of Schmalkalden, the major and minor catechisms of Luther and the *Formula Concordiae*. Scripture alone is recognized as infallible, while the formularies, though tested by the faith of so many generations, are not the last word, and must be corrected and completed.

Although Holy Scripture is the decisive authority in the Church it is nevertheless this Church that recognizes and proclaims this authority. In this way Scripture presupposes the Church while the Church lives wholly by the Scripture. The fact that Scripture presupposes the Church for its recognition brings with it the acceptance of an ecclesial tradition in which this supreme authority of Scripture is constantly reasserted as valid. The ecclesiastical formularies in particular are authoritative because they ensure and transmit the right understanding of the Gospel. The Church's preaching is authoritative because it leads to a constantly renewed understanding of the Gospel, suited to the age.

The relationship between Scripture, tradition and preaching is always subject to a certain tension that can only be borne if one believes in the Church, herself part of the contents of a faith engendered by Scripture. The theological reaction to this tension between Scripture and Tradition has not always been the same in the course of history. In our day there is a reaction against a too subjective interpretation of the axiom of "Scripture alone" and a growing appreciation of the tradition that has to transmit the Scriptures and a definite understanding of these Scriptures.

3. *Structure*

The Lutheran Churches do not all have the same inner structure. In Scandinavia they are administered by bishops, and the congregations are served by priests and deacons. In Austria and the Netherlands they are governed by presbyters and synods, while in Hungary the Lutherans have a bishop as well as elders. In Germany the Churches have been administered since 1945 by bishops, although they do not accept apostolic succession as essential to the Church.

Luther must be credited with having revived a sense of the general priesthood of all that are baptized, but neither he nor any of his followers has ever clearly defined the place of the officials who in fact have always functioned in the Lutheran Churches. Prof. Dr. W. J. Kooiman interprets Luther's opinion in the sense that every baptized Christian can administer both the word and the sacrament while professor Peter Meinhold maintains that Lutheran opinion in general reserves the function to those who are appointed to it on Christ's behalf. The latter declares, moreover, that there exists practically no theological examination of the ecclesiastical office in the Lutheran Churches. The concrete form of the office is accepted as determined or to be determined by historical circumstances.

4. *Distribution*

The total number of Lutheran Christians is estimated at about 75 million, which is almost one-third of Reformed Christendom. Their Churches are found principally in Germany, Scandinavia, Finland, Iceland, the Baltic States, Poland, Hungary, Austria, the Netherlands, Czechoslovakia, Rumania, France, the United States, Australia and as missionary Churches in India and Indonesia. Germany and the United States are considered to be the centers. These Churches have a strong sense of kinship. Since 1947, 61 Churches, spread over 32 countries, were affiliated to the Lutheran World Federation with a membership of about 50 million Lutherans.

5. *Spirituality*

The Lutheran religious attitude, rich in itself and deeply rooted, concentrates on the person, work and all-embracing grace of Jesus Christ. Consciousness of the redeemer's sanctifying activity here and now in every sincere believer has been carefully preserved as Luther's heritage. It finds expression in, among other things, the Lutherans' conviction of the Lord's real presence in the eucharist, in the specific devoutness of their numerous hymns and in their domestic worship. What St. Clement Hofbauer said in 1816 about the German Reformation is still typical of the Lutherans: "The Reformation came about because the Germans felt and still feel the need for piety; the Reformation spread and was maintained, not by heretics and philosophers, but by people who really wanted a religion that appealed to the heart." Finally, there arose in most Lutheran Churches a movement toward deeper reflection on, and more intense practice of, a sacramental and liturgical life. In this they consciously seek closer contact with the old, not yet divided Church.

6. Ecumenical Attitude

According to Lutheran conviction Christian unity would be sufficiently achieved if all Christians recognized Holy Scripture as the sole, decisive norm of faith and could agree on a common confession that would express this sole norm. Diversity in the exercise of ecclesiastical offices and in the forms of worship should be maintained. The common faith would find further expression in a synodal or conciliar arrangement.

Several Lutheran Churches have already united on this basis in the Netherlands and the United States. Apart from the Lutheran World Federation, already mentioned, several smaller federations have been formed.

The Lutheran bishop Nathan Söderblom (1866-1931) organized the first World Congress for Christian unity on "Life and Work" in Stockholm, in 1925, and another Lutheran bishop, Y. Brilioth (1891-1959) gathered for the first time important material for an ecumenical study of the eucharist. From the beginning, the Lutherans cooperated zealously in the preparation and the establishment of the World Council of Churches. The Swedish Church established intercommunion with the Church of England, and in 1934 the Church of Finland restored episcopacy, abolished in 1884, so that intercommunion with the Church of England could take place. In practice there is also intercommunion between the Lutheran Churches in France and the Netherlands and the Reformed (Calvinist) Churches in these countries.

The situation of the United Churches (*Unierte Kirchen*) in Germany is exceptional. There are about thirteen of them, in which Lutheran and Calvinist Churches have been united since the last century. These United Churches federated in 1948 with 13 Lutheran and 2 Calvinist Churches and formed the "Evangelical Church in Germany" (*Evangelische Kirche in Deutschland*), which acts as a unit in its relations with the outside but maintains each Church's autonomy within.

Lastly, in 1957, the Lutheran World Federation inaugurated an institute for the study of its relations with the Catholic Church. After the experiences at a provisional institute set up in Copenhagen, a permanent center of studies was opened in Strasbourg in 1965. It is under the direction of Dr. Vilmos Vatja, one of the Lutheran observers at Vatican Council II.

The Lutheran World Federation was represented at all sessions of the Council by three observers, while the Evangelical Church of Germany also had one of its own.

II

THE REFORMED CHURCHES

1. *The Name*

This name is given to 221 Churches whose denominational confession is derived from the reforms of Huldrych Zwingli (1523) and John Calvin (1532). The original disagreements between these two Reformers were overcome for a large part by the efforts of Zwingli's successor, John Bullinger, and Calvin in the *Consensus Tigurinus,* concluded at Zurich in 1549. The Churches that adhered to the principles of these Reformers called themselves "the Churches reformed according to the Word of God". In this article they are called "reformed" to correspond with "réformé" and "reformiert" (French and German use), but without referring explicitly to the "Gereformeerde Kerken" in the Netherlands which differ in organization and mentality from the "Nederlandse Hervormde Kerk" (Dutch Reformed Church), although they share the same type of confession and structure with the last named.

Because of their structure, which is based on presbyters or elders, these Churches are also called presbyterian. Insofar as these Churches send delegates to the synod, which is above the local congregations, they are also designated as presbyterial-synodic Churches. The term "reformed" is usual on the European Continent and in the mission Churches founded from there, while the Anglo-Saxon usage is "presbyterian".

2. Confession

According to the Reformed Christians the essence of the Church is simply defined as the "Church of the Word"; the Church arises from the common confession in heart, word and deed of God's Word as it is offered to the believer in Holy Scripture, and in this Scripture only.

According to Reformed opinion, the denominational formularies are derived from the written Word of God and serve only to lead the faithful back to this Word. In themselves they do not constitute a complete doctrine of faith but rather refer to the Scripture; they contain utterances on the faith, elicited by historical circumstances and therefore varying from Church to Church; they witness to Holy Scripture the authority of which they have proclaimed in certain definite historical situations and of which they demand recognition also at present without however binding individual congregations or faithful to these confessions.

These various Reformed confessions cannot, therefore, serve as a basis for Reformed unity in matters of doctrine as is the case with the Lutheran *Book of Concord*. Nor is there a canon of Reformed confessions recognized by all the Churches. The Reformed Churches look on these rather as utterances of witness than as doctrinal pronouncements. This witness, however, of these various formularies has the same tendency as such pronouncements. The most important confessional formularies are: the Geneva Catechism, the French, Scottish, Dutch (or Belgian) Confessions, the Heidelberg Catechism, the Five Points of Doctrine of Dordrecht and the Confession of Westminster. They all date from the 16th century, except the Five Points which were drawn up in 1619.

3. Structure

The Reformed Churches are governed locally by a group of elders, elected by the congregation. These elders appoint the preacher or "Minister of the Word" and are responsible for the manner in which he exercises his function. He presides over the congregation. His function is transmitted to him by the laying on of hands and the prayer of other preachers. Apart from the elders and preachers there are also deacons who share in the material administration of the community. The local communities are held together in "classes" which in turn constitute an ecclesiastical province or Church. The communities send delegates to meetings of these "classes", and these meetings or conferences send delegates to the provincial or general assembly. In Anglo-Saxon countries the term used is "General Assembly", in Germany "Landessynode", in the Netherlands and elsewhere "Generale Synode". This Assembly has the highest authority in matters of doctrine and discipline.

4. *Distribution*

The total number of Reformed Christians is thought to be about 41 million, nearly one-sixth of the Christians of the Reformation. Their Churches are spread over Switzerland, France, Belgium, the Netherlands, Scotland, England, Germany, Hungary, Czechoslovakia, the United States, Canada, Australia, New Zealand, South Africa and Indonesia, with some diaspora communities in Greece, Spain, Portugal and Denmark. Since 1875 most of these Churches have established relations with each other through a world federation, called "The Alliance of the Reformed Churches throughout the World Holding the Presbyterian Order".

5. *Spirituality*

By their adherence to the Word of God in both the Old and the New Testaments, Reformed Christians are influenced as much by the law as by the Gospel. In this they emphasize the absolute sovereignty of God. God first imposed his law on man and then gave him in the Gospel the strength to fulfill that law. Piety is predominantly theocentric and at the same time lives through "Jesus Christ as our only hope in life and in death" (*Heidelberg Catechism*).

Whereas Luther expressed the Reformed accent on faith by

emphasizing "fides fiducialis", through which and in which man seeks all salvation from God alone, Calvin expressed this same accent by stressing the divine transcendence and sovereignty. Whereas Luther opposed whatever might threaten "sola fide"—every way of thinking by which man might even suggest that salvation could be attained through his own effort—Calvin expressly rejected even any appearance of divinizing creatures and proclaimed the infinite chasm between God and man. Just as Luther, Calvin wanted engagement in the threefold "sola", *i.e.*, "sola scriptura, sola gratia, sola fide"—once summarized by Luther in "Christus solus"—but he expressly added "soli Deo gloria".

The Reformed worship is remarkable for its sobriety and may be adequately described as a service of the Word. The form of life and ethics shows a certain rigidity which has sometimes led to what is called puritanism. This introversive and preferably quiet piety inspired, however, an enduring and personal acquaintanceship with the Scriptures as well as a conscientious concern with preaching. The present revival of ecclesial awareness and the gradual spread of a liturgical and sacramental development are both hampered and yet deepened by this kind of piety.

6. *Ecumenical Attitude*

According to these Reformed Christians, unity, as wanted by Christ, would be restored if all communities accepted the Bible as the only and decisive norm for their confessional formularies, their various ways of worshiping and their different ways of organizing themselves. There is here ample room for pluriformity. In order to achieve this the already mentioned World Alliance encourages Churches of its own type to cooperate with each other, to become aware of how far they are already united, and it supports Churches inclined to establish some form of unity also in organization.

Many Reformed Churches participated from the beginning in the movement which led to the formation of the World Council of Churches, and the first Secretary General, Dr. W. A. Visser 't Hooft, is a Calvinist. During the last century some unity with intercommunion was achieved with Lutheran Churches and the Lutheran Federation was formed. The Presbyterian World Alliance sent three observers to Vatican Council II, while the Secretariat for Christian Unity invited four other prominent members of the Calvinist Churches, who had consistently given to understand that they were striving for better relations with the Catholic Church.

III

THE ANGLICAN CHURCHES

1. *Name*

The 43 Churches of this type originated, directly or indirectly, in the 16th-century Reformation in England (in 1534, called "Ecclesia Anglicana" by Henry VIII). The names of the individual Churches usually refer to the countries in which they are found, such as the Church of England, the Church of Ireland, the Churches of India, Pakistan, Burma and Ceylon. In some cases the name expresses an element close to faith, as that of The Episcopal Church of Scotland, The Protestant Episcopal Church in the U.S.A., The Holy Catholic Church of Japan and The Holy Catholic Church of China. The use of the definite articles in these titles expresses the idea that there is only one Church of Christ, which, however, takes on a specific national form in each land.

2. *Confession*

The Anglican Churches have no confessional formulary in the strict sense. In principle, they abide by the Holy Scriptures, the creeds of the early Church, the Book of Common Prayer (1549, revised in 1552 and 1559) with its catechism for confirmation candidates and the 39 Articles of Religion (1562). It is rather the Book of Common Prayer that the Anglican considers as representative of his confession, even more than the series of 39 articles. In England there was no Reformer of the caliber of Calvin or Luther to shape the character of the Reformation there.

The Reformation was primarily effected in the liturgical and Church-law sectors of the life of the Church. In the area of dogma, Holy Scripture is formally the source and highest norm. Its authoritative interpretation may be found in the Fathers of the early centuries and the doctrinal decisions of the first four ecumenical councils. The ecumenical creeds have a place in the liturgy although the so-called Athanasian creed is not obligatory.

In England the "Ecclesia Anglicana" has wanted to hold on to the tradition of the early Church more consciously and explicitly than on the Continent and has desired to limit itself to the expurgation of what it considered to be late-medieval deformations. On the other hand, the English Reformation demonstrably shows Lutheran and Calvinist influence. The Anglican type of Church has always tried to contain both what it considered as Catholic and what it considered as Reformed tendencies within its communion, and it has developed a tradition of tolerant comprehensiveness.

In the matters of doctrine it distinguishes between fundamental and non-fundamental articles of faith. What is necessary for salvation is considered fundamental and as such to be contained in the Scriptures. In non-fundamental matters there is a preference for freedom of opinion and freedom of practice. Widely spread is the opinion that no single Church is the only guardian of the apostolic tradition and that the term "Catholic" applies to all Churches faithful to the belief of the early creeds and councils, to the administration of the sacraments and to the episcopal office as prolongation of the apostolic office.

In regard to interpretation, it is often said of Anglicans that they gladly call upon "sound reasoning and thus are always open for contemporary ideas and especially flexible in practical applications.

3. Structure

The Anglican Churches recognize the threefold ministry of bishop, priest and deacon. In ecumenical contacts with other Churches they have stressed the significance of apostolic suc-

cession. Recently, though, some Anglicans have said that episcopacy does indeed belong to the fullness (*plene esse*) of the
Church but that its absence does not necessarily rule out the
essential presence (*esse*) of the Church. The Anglo-Catholic
wing looks on the Church's structure more or less in the same
way as the Catholic and the Eastern Orthodox Churches, while
the "evangelical" wing shows more affinity with the Lutheran
and Calvinist types of Churches. The Evangelicals accept episcopacy as a historically justified form of ministry, but they do
not consider it necessary.

Since 1867 sixteen Anglican Churches have formed the "Anglican Communion" for the sake of closer mutual links. These
Churches enjoy complete autonomy but their bishops meet about
once in every ten years for consultation under the honorary
presidency of the Archbishop of Canterbury in the Lambeth
Conferences which issue collective encyclicals and resolutions.

4. *Distribution*

The Church of England has given rise to numerous national
and autonomous Churches, Church provinces and dioceses.
These are not only found in countries at present or formerly in-
cluded in the British Commonwealth but all over the world, apart
from the Soviet Union and Greenland. The number of Anglicans
is estimated at about 30 million, or about one-seventh of the
total of Reformed Christians. Next to the Church of England the
Protestant Episcopal Church in the U.S.A. is also an important
center of Anglican life.

5. *Spirituality*

The differences between the Anglo-Catholic stream and the
Evangelical one show not only in doctrinal matters but also in
their piety. The former group tends to be more sacramental- and
liturgical-minded, while the latter shows a preference for preaching and the reading of Scripture. Both use the Book of Common
Prayer and the vast collection of hymns according to their own
theological inclination. Both thrive on a long and rich religious

tradition, revived by the Tractarian Movement of Keble, Newman and Pusey and by the "Evangelical Revivals" of the last
century. Anglican worship therefore combines an unforced feeling for fixed forms with hymns and silent prayers of remarkable earnestness.

6. *Ecumenical Attitude*

After various individual initiatives the third Lambeth Conference of 1888 already concerned itself with ecumenical problems. It adopted a proposal made by the Protestant Episcopal
Church in the U.S.A. which had drawn up a basis for discussions
on reunion in 1886 at Chicago. Known since as the "(Chicago-)
Lambeth Quadrilateral", it contained the following points: (a)
the recognition of Scripture "as the witness of God's self-revela-
tion to man and as the rule and ultimate norm of faith"; (b) the
Nicene Creed "as an adequate affirmation of the Christian faith,
or the Apostles' Creed as used in baptism"; (c) "the divinely in-
stituted sacraments of baptism and communion, as expressing
for all the common life of the universal brotherhood in and with
Christ"; and (d) "a ministry, recognized throughout the Church
as sanctioned, not only by the inward call of the Holy Spirit but
also by Christ's commission and the authority of the whole body
of the Church".

Since the middle of the last century there has been frequent
contact between the Church of England and individual Orthodox
Churches. These were followed by discussions with the Old
Catholics, episcopally governed Lutheran Churches, Presbyterian
Churches and the Catholic Church. Charles Brent (1862-1929),
Anglican Bishop of the Philippine Islands, promoted the move-
ment of Faith and Order.

Many of those who were prominent in paving the way for
bringing to existence and inspiring to the present day both the
International Board of Missions and the World Council of
Churches were Anglicans. In all this the idea prevailed that the
Anglican Church-type could mediate as a "bridge-chuck" be-
tween Catholic and Reformed types, inasmuch as it contains ele-

ments of both in itself. Consequently, the *pietas anglicana* and the typically English sense of practical possibilities have, with the actual world extension of the "Anglican Communion", contributed greatly to the present ecumenical situation and the positive relations between very many Churches. The visits of the Archbishop of Canterbury in Constantinople, Rome and Moscow continued a tradition of Anglican initiative in this matter. At Vatican Council II were three Anglican observers in addition to a personal representative of the Archbishops of Canterbury and York.

IV

THE BAPTIST CHURCHES

1. *Name*

The name is a collective one and today covers two main streams. The first group consists of fraternities, communities or societies of Mennonites (Dutch: *Doopsgezinden*). These sprang from a radical reform movement at the beginning of the 16th century called Anabaptists, gathered together by Menno Simons (1536). The names refer either to their first organizer or to their insistence on adult baptism (Ana-baptist = Re-baptizer).

The second group consists of Churches or Unions of Baptists. In England they arose among the independent and puritan reformers of the beginning of the 17th century. These, too, reject infant baptism and maintain that only an adult, confessing the faith, can be baptized. Historical data to prove a connection between the origins of these two main streams are lacking.

2. *Confession*

Both groups belong to the "Free Church" type and refuse to conform to any form of "establishment" in religion, whether based on nationality or on a specific confessional formulary. Both also share as their distinctive religious conviction that baptism can only be administered to adults who are personally responsible for their confession of faith. The only authoritative norm for this confession is Scripture. They recognize no confessional formularies, but inherited through their original environment certain influences from the Reformation and a great respect for the Apostolic Creed. Lastly, the Mennonites also show a strong sense of eschatological expectation.

3. Structure

Both groups live in autonomous communities without rigid organization. In principle every member is entitled to administer the Word and the sacrament, but in fact it is only done by properly trained ministers. Many communities have federated among themselves but this federation has no more than a purely advisory capacity in matters of doctrine and discipline and the communities remain autonomous.

4. Distribution

Mennonites are found in the Netherlands, Western Germany, France, with the largest representation in the United States and Canada. Their number is about 671,000. The largest number of Baptists is found in the United States (18 million), but there are large groups in the United Kingdom, the Soviet States and, as missionary groups, in Burma and India, among others. The total number of this type of Baptists is certainly above 40 million, or about one-sixth of the Reformed Christians. This number should be rated higher since the children of Baptist families are not counted, as not yet baptized.

5. Spirituality

Both groups attach more value to sanctification on the basis of a personal evangelical faith than on that of dogma and ecclesiastical institutions. Their ideal is the "living community", the "holy community of those baptized again according to the example of the apostles". The personal confession of faith at baptism is considered of primary importance, and although they stand for elasticity in the government of the community, they like to see an efficient discipline in the congregation to deal with cases of unchristian conduct. They also look on the community of the faithful as a community that affects every aspect of life, and here tolerance and charity in service are the decisive factors. Both groups were influenced by the pietist movement in their spirituality.

Mennonites are inclined to avoid secular involvement, and for this reason decline to take part in government, reject the taking of oaths and are opposed to military service. On the other hand, they share in work for peace and take part in pacifist movements. The more conservative among them prefer simple and sometimes old-fashioned dress and reject modern comforts.

The ethical and devout attitude of the Baptists is somewhat similar but they are less opposed to taking part in public life and do not refuse to accept office in government. Characteristic of their piety is the famous *Pilgrim's Progress* of John Bunyan (died in 1688) which is still being translated and constantly republished. Meditative prayer occupies an important place in their meetings.

The literary work of the Baptist poet John Milton is illustrative, *e.g.,* his *Paradise Lost* (1667) and *Paradise Regained* (1671), while in our time can be mentioned the evangelist activity of Billy Graham.

6. *Ecumenical Attitude*

Their longing for unity does not extend far but is quite serious. It is directed toward a kind of federated union of otherwise independent communities or groups of communities. Within their specific Church-type there already exist various unions, "conventions" and "conferences".

The Baptist World Alliance comprises more than 11 million members. Some federations are members of the World Council of Churches while others are fearful of too strong ecclesial bonds. In general, the Baptists have always been interested in missionary work and showed themselves always ready for practical cooperation in this field. It was the Baptist William Carey (1761-1834) who started the missionary movement among Reformed Christians. Already before 1810 he suggested the setting up of an international and inter-Church missionary conference. His proposal, however, did not materialize until the World Missionary Conference was convened at Edinburgh in 1910. This Conference is taken as the beginning of the ecumenical movement today.

The World Convention of the Churches of Christ ("Disciples of Christ"), a community closely related to the Baptists (1827) intended from its beginning the realization of Christian unity but on the basis of only the Word and baptism. They plead for a Church unity in which room is left for the Catholic, Presbyterian and Congregationalist types. Representing this World Convention was also an observer at Vatican Council II.

The Mennonites (in Dutch the "Doopsgezinden") are oriented toward a predominantly spiritual unity; only the Dutch and German fraternities belong to the World Council of Churches.

V

THE CONGREGATIONALIST CHURCHES

1. Name

This type of Church polity sprang from the puritan sector of the English Reformation. Some people opposed the episcopalism of the Church of England and the presbyterianism of the Church of Scotland with the autonomy of the local "congregation". This word does not refer so much to the sociological aspect as to a gathering for the purpose of worship. Insofar as these people insisted on being independent of the established Church, they are also called Independents.

2. Confession

Although at the beginning sectarian and spiritual tendencies prevailed, the religious opinions of the Reformation are predominant today. The Congregationalist Churches have no confessional formulary that binds them all together, but in general they follow the Westminster Confession except where this Confession limits the autonomy of the congregations. Both the English and the American Congregationalists issued formularies of minor importance. The Protestant approach of the communities varies from the strictly orthodox to the latitudinarian or "liberal" (in the continental sense of the word).

3. *Structure*

The local community itself has the function of mediating between God and man. It is to this community that Christ and his Spirit make known God's will. The communities elect their own ministers and give them the necessary mandate for the administration of Word and sacrament. Sometimes these ministers function like the bishops in other Churches, and their associations or unions sometimes act as the council of elders in other denominations. The basic principle, however, remains that the Spirit is primarily and essentially active in the gathering of the faithful, and the specific functions arise from the general priesthood of the faithful.

4. *Distribution*

Communities of this ecclesial type are found mainly in Great Britain and the United States. Total membership is estimated at 5 million.

5. *Spirituality*

This is mainly characterized by a puritan, sober form of worship, personal acquaintance with the Scriptures, the high demands put on the minister of the Word and the rejection of all authority outside that of the community itself. The religious is marked by great confidence in the strength of the Holy Spirit in both the individual faithful and in the gathering of the community.

6. *Ecumenical Attitude*

Congregationalists aim at wide mutual tolerance of the autonomous communities each with their own confession, form of worship and government. Federation is desired in view of practical cooperation but not as a preparation for possible reunion. Nevertheless, there is a tendency toward closer mutual contact with regular meetings of delegates of individual communities, and several "unions" have been arranged. All Congregationalist associations are now united in the International Congregational Council, founded in 1891, but not properly organized until 1949.

From the beginning Congregationalists have taken part in ecumenical activities and they are at home in the complex relationships of the World Council of Churches because this Council leaves every Church its own integrity. The Congregationalists sent five observers to Vatican Council II.

VI

THE METHODIST CHURCHES

1. Name

This type of Church sprang from a pietistic revivalist movement in the Church of England during the 18th century. It was inaugurated by the brothers, John and Charles Wesley, who aimed at deeper personal conversion and sanctification by means of Bible meetings, more frequent celebration of the Lord's supper, visits to those that are sick or in prison, and preaching of the Gospel to the masses. Their strict methodical application to inner piety seems to have given rise to the title "Methodists", which was accepted by their followers. The movement found itself gradually outside the Church of England, and developed a more institutional character. Since 1891 it has presented itself as "Church" and established itself in the United States in the shape of autonomous Churches.

2. Confession

From the doctrinal point of view the Methodists on the whole more or less accept the 39 Articles of Religion of the Church of England, which they have reduced to 25, without any essential changes. Their worship is taken for a decisive part from the Book of Common Prayer. Some Methodist Churches veer toward Lutheranism in matters of penance, grace and sanctification.

3. *Structure*

Methodist Churches are strictly organized and are sometimes compared with the Catholic Church from this point of view. The American Churches and various others have adopted an episcopal structure, though the British ones are more presbyterian in organization. All their Churches have, moreover, presbyters or elders and deacons. While elders and deacons receive ordination (*ordinatio*), bishops and deaconesses only receive a blessing. In America the original leaders were Anglican priests, but these were later called "superintendents" and lastly "bishops". The British Methodists stopped at presbyters and gave supreme ecclesiastical authority to the "Conference". Apostolic succession is not considered a matter of Church Order, and the functional distinction between bishops and presbyters is looked on as a matter for practical consideration. Moreover, sometimes lay members are entrusted with the function of preaching, but not with that of administering the sacraments.

4. *Distribution*

The Methodist Churches constitute the most important ecclesial foundation that issued from Anglicanism. They not only influenced the whole Church in the United States but also the mother Church in England. They also developed greater missionary activity than any other European Church. They are mainly found in the English-speaking regions of the world but also in Brazil and Mexico and as smaller Churches in Middle-European and Scandinavian countries. The total membership is thought to be about 30 million, of which more than 12 million is in the United States.

5. *Spirituality*

Their spiritual life is nourished by the liturgical traditions of Anglicanism as well as by the devout inheritance of the pietistic movement. Along with forms and texts of the ancient Christian liturgy the Methodists possess hundreds of hymns of a powerful devotional character. Their tradition has incorporated the Wesleyan emphasis on personal sanctification as well as the Wesleyan demand that each member should seek perfection in love. The plan of "escaping from the coming vengeance and being redeemed from sin" was further set out by John Wesley (1703-1791) in his "Rules": "Leave evil, do good and be faithful to the ordinances of God." The first rule encompasses the rejection of a worldly life, drunkenness, quarrels, usury, smuggling, self-love, irresponsible borrowing, while one must spare others what would be unwelcome to oneself. The second rule encourages the giving of alms, the visiting of the sick and prisoners, the education of the ignorant, a busy and moderate life, helpfulness toward fellow-Christians, the taking up of the cross of self-denial and the acceptance of the world's ridicule. The third rule concerns participation in Church-service, the practice of prayer (private and familial) and familiarity with the Holy Scriptures and fasting.

The psychological elements of experience and feeling as a witness of the new life that the Holy Spirit awakens in the believer are particularly valued; illustrative is their well-known song "Jesus, Lover of My Soul". Everywhere they show themselves keen on evangelization, mission work and social help. They played an important part in the abolition of slavery. In the same way Methodism brought forth the Salvation Army (1865).

6. *Ecumenical Attitude*

Their approach to reunion resembles that of the Anglicans, except in that they have never considered the matter of episcopacy as urgent or essential. Although many divisions took place during the last century, many internal reunions have been achieved in the last thirty years. Most Methodist Churches have been brought together in the World Methodist Council, in 1951, on the basis of a common confession. From the beginning the Methodists have cooperated in the preparation and organization of the World Missionary Council and the World Council of

Churches. One prominent member of this group was John R. Mott (1865-1955), president of the World Mission Congress at Edinburgh in 1910 and, afterward, of the International Council of Missions. The Methodist show great willingness for all ecumenical contacts and they seem to be especially sensitive to the spiritual and missionary aspects of the effort for reconciliation. They had also three observers at Vatican Council II.

VII

UNITED CHURCHES

The ecumenical movement brought about new types of Churches that are as yet difficult to define. They arose out of unions of Churches of a different character without any of them abandoning entirely their own characteristics.

The United Church of Canada came about in 1925 through the union of Presbyterians, Congregationalists, Methodists and an already existing bloc of united autonomous communities. They arrived at a common confession to which all made their contribution. Since all four groups were presbyterian in character it was sufficient for the structure to accept some accidental mutual adjustments.

The Church of Christ in China was set up in 1927 and united Baptist, Congregationalist, Methodist and Presbyterian Churches, as well as a missionary foundation of the United Church of Canada, the United Brethren in Christ and some autonomous communities. They agreed on the contents of a common confession, but reserved freedom in the wording of it. There was no difficulty about structure, since all had a presbyterian organization.

The Church of Christ in Japan came about in 1940 under compulsion by the State, and united Presbyterians, Methodists, Congregationalists, Baptists, Anglicans and Lutherans. When this compulsion was lifted in 1945, the Anglicans and Lutherans withdrew. The other groups have not succeeded in achieving a genuine inner unity and whether this union will continue to exist is not certain.

The Church of South India is without doubt the most remarkable united Church. It was set up in 1947 when Episcopalian, Presbyterian and Congregationalist Churches united. There is unity of confession, of worship and of ministry. Insofar as the ministry is concerned, the typical contribution of each of the three groups was taken as constitutive: the congregation, the presbyter and the bishop. This development is being closely followed by many because an attempt has been made here to overcome one of the most fundamental barriers to reunion.

There is an outlook of a similar development in North India and Pakistan, on Ceylon and in Nigeria, Ghana and Australia. In Australia there are Congregationalists, Methodists and Presbyterians in concert, and the remarkable fact is that they search for admission to the tradition of the historical episcopate, and that from the Church of South India. Lastly the Church of South India also sent an observer to Vatican Council II.

VIII

THE SECTARIAN TYPE OF CHURCH

It is very important in ecumenical discussion to distinguish between the types of Churches which derived from the Reformation and the sectarian type. In general those Christian groups are considered "sects" which interpret the Bible in a very literal sense, tend to concentrate exclusively on only one or a few aspects of the Christian faith, lay exceptional claims to individual enlightenment or revelation by the Holy Spirit, and are tense with the emotional expression of such individual experiences.

Today many sects share an exclusive concentration on their belief in an imminent and sensational return of the Lord, announced, according to them, by many signs. Followers of these sects also live in a strongly emotional opposition to existing Churches; they emphasize a closely knit social life and mutual assistance, are aggressive and readily face sacrifices. The appeal of their preaching often lies in their radicalism and lack of compromise; their courage often causes admiration but their methods often cause astonishment.

The most important sects today are: various groups of Adventists, Darbyites or the Assembly of God, Mormons or Latter Day Saints, the Pentecostal Movement, Irvingites or Catholic Apostolic Churches, Jehovah's Witnesses. All these movements originated in the United States except the Irvingites who are British in origin.

Sects that cannot really be called Christian are: the Unitarians (English and American), the Universalists of the United States, the Free Catholic Church (linked with the Theosophic Movement) and the Christian Scientists (from Great Britain and the United States).

These sects are as much a problem for the Protestant Churches as for the Roman Catholic Church. In their dialogue with Catholics the Protestants rightly dissociate themselves from these sects because the Protestant Churches do not merely live in opposition to the Catholic Church as the sects do. Protestants are vitally concerned with *the* Church and consciously live on salvation as mediated by the Church. The differences between Reformed Christians and Catholics are ultimately a matter of how the Church exists, as is clear from the origin of the Reformation which consciously set out to reform the Church. The dialogue between Catholics and Reformed Christians must therefore be about the essence and shape of Christ's one Church. The understanding and realization of this one Church demands that they exchange insight and experience.[4]

[4] K. Hutten, *Geloof en sekte; het sectarisme als anti-reformatorisch geloofsverschijnsel* (Franeker, 1958).

PART IV

CHRONICLE OF THE LIVING CHURCH

In Collaboration with
Katholiek Archief
Amersfoort, Netherlands

World Council of Churches

Report of the General Secretary to the Central Committee (Enugu, Nigeria, Jan., 1965)

I

THE SPIRIT OF THE PIONEERS

This is the time to remember the pioneers of the ecumenical movement, the men who had the spiritual imagination and the courage to create the movements which joined their forces in the World Council of Churches. For Bishop Brent, the father of Faith and Order, was born in 1862, Dr. John R. Mott, the father of the International Missionary Council, in 1865, and Archbishop Nathan Söderblom, the father of Life and Work, in 1866. Each of them had his own background and calling. Brent, the Anglican; Mott the Methodist; Söderblom the Lutheran: Brent pastor, missionary and fighter against social evils; Mott layman, evangelist and Christian strategist; Söderblom theologian, church leader and peacemaker. But they had also a great deal in common. And what they had in common is a precious part of our heritage. I would mention especially four aspects of their life-work.

(a) They were men with a truly catholic concern for the life of all the Churches. Some of us remember that Mott used to speak of the spiritual debt he owed to all Churches and particularly to the Orthodox Churches and to the Quakers. Mott and Söderblom were both leaders of the historic meeting of the World's Student Christian Federation held in 1911 at Constantinople which was attended by many representatives of the Eastern Churches, including the Rev. Germanos Strinopoulos, later Archbishop Germanos, Exarch of the Ecumenical Patriarchate and one of the first Presidents of the World Council. The meeting was described as the first one at which the ancient Eastern Churches were brought in touch with the emerging ecumenical movement. Brent who had worked in the area of the younger Churches made his contact with the older Churches in 1920 when the Orthodox delegation came to the preliminary meeting of Faith and Order in Geneva, and wrote at that time: "We of the West need the fragrant, graceful worship of the East." All three had a capacity for appreciating genuine Christian faith in members of other Churches. Söderblom surprised a sophisticated American dinner audience by giving a solo performance of the Sankey hymn: "There Were Ninety-and-Nine", but he was also the man who did everything possible to bring Orthodox delegations to the Stockholm Conference. Brent felt at home in the evangelical atmosphere of the Edinburgh Conference of 1910, but tried also his very best to interest Roman Catholic bishops and theologians in Faith and Order. Mott used the same language in addressing the first sobor of the Orthodox Church of Russia in 1917 as he did in speaking to the World Conference of Christian Youth in Amsterdam in 1939.

(b) So they refused to let themselves be imprisoned in any one particular section of Church life. Brent played his great role in the Lausanne Faith and Order Conference, but participated with equal energy in the World Missionary Conference in Edinburgh and in the Life and Work Conference in Stockholm. Mott was of course involved in all ecumenical movements; founder of the World's Student Christian Federation and the International Missionary Council, presiding officer at the Oxford Life and Work Conference, chairman of section in the Edinburgh Faith and Order Conference, Honorary President of the World Council of

Churches. Söderblom was not only the soul of Life and Work but an active leader in Faith and Order.

(c) All three had a passionate concern for unity, but that concern was not for unity for its own sake. They sought unity for the sake of the fulfillment of the Church's mandate in the world. Brent and Mott emphasized especially the missionary motive. Söderblom proclaimed in the midst of World War I that the unity of Christians should be realized in order that the Church could be the conscience of the nations. They were at one in setting the question of unity in the wider setting of the Church's calling and mandate in and to the whole needy world.

(d) All three stood for the renewal of the life of the Churches. They saw the need for a new obedience in a new situation. And so they sought to create new structures for new tasks. They knew that unity does not come by the addition of existing institutional forms but by the common response of the Churches to the Holy Spirit and their common transformation. Mott sought to "liberate the lay-forces", as he called it, and appealed to the Churches to take their missionary task seriously. Söderblom asked whether the Churches must sit fearfully in their houses without faith and without courage and called them to discover together their prophetic ministry. Brent wrote during World War I: "The world is falling to pieces, the Churches are tugging behind the armies and nothing is being done that is worthy of the name of witness-bearing for unity as Christ begs us to interpret it."

II

FOUR CRITERIA

We are not called to imitate these pioneers in every respect. But these elements of their work and message: true catholicity, dedication to the whole task of the Church, unity for the sake of the Church's mission in the world, readiness for a renewal of life, these remain part and parcel of the life of the World Council. And in these four respects we have yet far to go.

True Catholicity

We have reached a point in the membership of the World Council at which our catholocity has deeply impressive possibilities. But it is still a potential catholicity. It has yet to be worked out and applied in the life of our Churches. We shall only be truly catholic if we arrive at such a caring and sharing that the Churches of East and West, of North and South, the young and the old, the small and the great, bear each other's burdens and expect eagerly to receive spiritual gifts from each other.

Dedication to the Whole Task of the Church

The World Council's work now covers many areas and concerns, but there are as yet too many people in our Churches who are only for the specific concern of one particular division or department and too few who seek to understand and support the whole and who realize that it is only in their togetherness that our various types of work reflect the calling of the Church.

Unity for the Sake of the Church's Mission to the World

Here again we have a new opportunity since the integration of the World Council of Churches and the International Missionary Council. But the real task is still before us. We have only begun to ask what it means that the Church is called to mission and service in six continents and that the local congregation must have a missionary and not merely a conserving structure.

Readiness for Renewal of Life

Renewal means change and change means the giving up of patterns and structures which are no longer able to meet the need of the hour. It is therefore to be expected that there will always be tension between those who stand for renewal and those who would maintain existing structures. And it is not a foregone conclusion that every proposal for renewal is necessarily right. What is needed is that this tension be accepted as a constructive tension and that it does not lead to a hardening of opposite positions. The World Council must be willing and able to live with that tension in its own life. As a World Council of *Churches* it takes the existing structures seriously; as an ecumenical movement it must also stand for that renewal which is the condition of advance toward unity.

III

SOLIDARITY IN AN INTERDEPENDENT WORLD

One of the most important items on the agenda of this meeting of the Central Committee is the preparation of the World Conference on Church and Society which we hope to hold in 1966. The World Council has always been concerned about social and international questions and they have had an important place in our deliberation. But this will be the first time since the creation of the World Council, in fact, the first time since the Oxford Conference on Church, Community and State in 1937, that we will have a large world conference specifically devoted to these issues.

It is not difficult to see why we need such a confrontation. There have always been social problems, but in our time the basic problem of overcoming hunger or poverty and of social justice has become the issue which dominates all other issues and on the solution of which the future of mankind depends. The interdependence of our modern world, the conviction that the needs of all can be met, the emergence of a new sense of dignity and a new hope among underprivileged masses, the emergence of so many new nations which desire to build healthy national societies—all these have made the international, intercontinental social problem the most inescapable issue of our time. As we meet in Africa many of us will be made even more conscious of its reality than we were before.

Now the Christian Churches have a very specific responsibility in this field. They live in all these societies. They want to bear their burdens and to share in the task of nation-building. They are, through their work of mission and service, already deeply involved in the attempt to meet the most crying needs of the developing nations. But they also know those more far-crying needs of the developing nations. But they know also that more, far more, is needed, namely a great awakening of the spirit of human solidarity so that new structures of international and economic cooperation may be created and a concerted attack may be made on hunger and poverty.

So the question is firstly a spiritual question. Are we our brother's keepers? The question of my neighbor's bread is not a material but a spiritual question, said Nicolai Berdyaev. The secret of solidarity is the secret of men living together as fellow-creatures and brothers for all of whom Christ died.

Very many people have not yet understood the gravity of the responsibility which our generation bears in this respect. It is disquieting that in many countries the reaction to recent political developments has been to decrease rather than to increase the willingness to participate in plans for international assistance. Even in our own Churches we have not yet created that awareness of the needs of other peoples and that readiness for large-scale and costly action without which no real advance is possible. Our World Council must show the way, not allow the tension between rich and poor to become an unbridgeable chasm, and help the Churches to work for the revolutionary change in thought and action by which we can overcome social and national egoism and establish genuine solidarity between the peoples.

The World Conference on Church and Society can and must become an important step toward that goal.

IV

RELATIONS WITH THE ROMAN CATHOLIC CHURCH

When I turn next to the relations between the World Council of Churches and the Roman Catholic Church I must begin by saying that I find it this time more difficult to speak on this subject than on any previous occasion. The reason is of course that recent developments, particularly those in the last days of the third session of the Vatican Council, have created a sense of great uncertainty.

On the one hand, we cannot and must not underestimate the strength of the movement for a true spiritual renewal which is at work in the Roman Catholic Church, and which has found expression in many of the speeches and some of the actions of the Council. We know by experience that there is a great difference between the wish for renewal and its actual application in daily Church-life. But we must rejoice that there is so much new thinking, so much readiness to face anew the issues of the task and message of the Church in the modern world and that this new approach is to such a large extent inspired by a new listening to the biblical witness.

On the other hand, we find that this renewal meets with powerful opposition in leading ecclesiastical circles. This has happened especially with regard to a number of matters which are of great moment for inter-Church relationships. The result so far is that while in certain respects the Council has come to decisions which from an ecumenical point of view are constructive, it has postponed decision on other important matters, such as religious liberty, and in some cases only reaffirmed the old positions.

The question now arises: What should be our attitude at this time when there is reason for both expectation and disappointment? It seems to me that we ought to keep in mind the following considerations:

First of all we cannot forget that in our own Churches we have by no means solved the problem of the tension between the forces of renewal and the existing structures. Secondly, just as many Roman Catholics and members of other Churches rejoice together when they see in each other's Churches signs of genuine spiritual renewal and are thus brought into a new relation to each other, so the anxiety about developments which put obstacles in the way to renewal is an anxiety in which many Roman

Catholics and many Christians of other confessions share, so that there is a sense of being involved in a common cause. Thirdly, the adoption and promulgation of the Decree on Ecumenism creates a new situation. It means that the Roman Catholic Church is no longer standing apart. It expresses its desire to enter into fraternal relations with other Churches. It does so on the basis of a conception of ecumenism which differs in important respects from the conceptions of ecumenism held in our midst, but the fact remains that it desires to enter into conversation with other Churches since it recognizes that in those Churches Christ is working. Now this surely means that the Roman Catholic Church and the non-Roman Catholic Churches bear a great responsibility for each other. Through the developments of recent years they have become more than ever "their brother's keepers".

Is it not already clear that we have in fact exerted a great, as it were, subterranean influence upon each other? Has not the ecumenical movement been an important factor in the new development in the Roman Catholic Church? And have we not received important spiritual stimulation from the Roman Catholic ecumenists? Or if we look at the world situation, is it not clear that we are together faced with the obligation to reinterpret the task of the Church in an increasingly secularized world and to find the prophetic word to remind men in their disorder of the order of God? A mere polite and passive coexistence is not enough. There must be the acceptance of responsibility of each other and therefore an intensive conversation. Is it necessary to say that such a conversation does not mean that deep convictions will be silenced or minimized? Insofar as this dialogue has to do with the specific issues of doctrine it will of course take place between the Roman Catholic Church and other Churches. From the point of view of the World Council it is normal and necessary that such inter-Church discussions shall take place, if and when the Churches are ready for them. Insofar as the dialogue has to do with matters in which the World Council itself is competent, the dialogue can take place between the Roman Catholic Church and the W.C.C.

Our task is to work out a clear distinction between these two types of dialogue.

V

THE SIGNIFICANCE OF REGIONAL ECUMENICAL DEVELOPMENTS

A word should be said about regional ecumenical developments. During these last few years the process of bringing together the Churches on a regional level has made much progress. It is noteworthy that now that such a development is also under way in Latin America, regional bodies exist in practically every continent.

But the significance of these regional organizations for the life of the ecumenical movement is not always understood. Thus it has recently been suggested that their growth is a sign of the disintegration of the ecumenical movement. Such a view reveals a great ignorance of the motives and factors which operate in this field. As the World Council seeks to promote the growth of regional bodies it is not digging its own grave. On the contrary. Ecumenicity begins at home; in the *oikos* of the Churches. But today when continents become realities in a way that was not true in the past, when they face specific common problems that differ from those of other continents, continental councils become an important link in the total ecumenical chain. Their first task is to serve the Christian Churches in their own region and continent. They help the Churches to solve problems that must be solved on a regional level. They can be the spokesmen of the Churches to the various governmental regional organizations. As an example, one thinks of the very important role which the All Africa Conference of Churches has to play in relation to the planning of new structures for education in Africa.

But they can also render a very great service to the World Council. They bring to it the voice of their continent. One thinks of the very great significance of the plans made by the East Asia

Christian Conference for the conference on "the confession of the Christian faith in Asia today". They call the attention of the World Council to the specific needs of their areas. And they can act as channels for communication and action for the World Council. Thus, the large "Ecumenical Program for Emergency Action in Africa" has been worked out in consultation between the W.C.C. and the A.A.C.C. and its success will to a large extent depend on the establishment of close cooperation between the two.

There is no desire on the part of the W.C.C. to interfere in any way with the autonomy of the regional bodies. For the W.C.C. is by its very structure and constitution forbidden to do so. But we have a strong desire to work out relationships of cooperation with all regional bodies which are willing to cooperate with us.

The "New Situation" between Rome and the Reformed Churches

It is not likely that Geneva will create an "Avenue du 18ᵐᵉ Février 1965" in spite of the historic event which took place on that date in that city. It is true that because of the pace with which we move today, the word "historic" is often associated with the cynical slant of "soon forgotten" or "already belonging to yesterday". But February 18, 1965 is here called an historic date because this event marked a turning point in history. And this turn concerns a "new situation"—the expression actually used—in the relationship between Rome and the Protestant Churches.

To start with, we should remember that Saturday, November 21, 1964, saw the solemn promulgation of the long expected Conciliar Decree on Ecumenism. However, at the eleventh hour some alterations were imposed from above. No further discussion was allowed and the implication's were so painful for both the Council Fathers and the observers that they dampened the joy with which this solemn promulgation should have been received by the Church at large and all Churches in particular. There was genuine anxiety about how the other Churches would receive this decree.

The first answer to this question came soon enough. During the annual meeting of the Central Committee of the World

Council of Churches, held at Enugu, Nigeria (January 12-21, 1965), the resigning Secretary-General of the W.C.C., Dr W. A. Visser 't Hooft, dealt extensively—should we not sincerely and gratefully say "magnanimously"—with the present relationship between the W.C.C. and the Roman Catholic Church. (See text pp. 167-8.)

Report on the Council by Dr. Lukas Vischer

At the same meeting of the Central Committee of the World Council of Churches, the Swiss minister, Dr. Lukas Vischer, who is the World Council's accredited observer at Vatican Council II, reported in detail on the third session as a whole. In his conclusion Dr. Vischer stated that the third session gives a confused picture of what is going on in the Roman Catholic Church. The separated Churches cannot observe this coldly, still less look on what has taken place as if it meant a defeat of Rome and in a sense a victory for themselves. Once again, the Churches should be aware of their responsibility for each other. It is clear from the Decree on Ecumenism that the Roman Catholic Church is resolutely determined to engage in an ecumenical dialogue. This demands an answer from the separated Churches. How should it be done? The decree does not say how the separated Churches can join in a common dialogue or in common activity. This all-important question must be the subject with which the dialogue should start, according to Dr. Vischer.

A Common Working Committee

As a contribution to the question put by Dr. Vischer the Central Committee of the W.C.C. has passed a Recommendation which would lead to a practical beginning of this dialogue between the W.C.C. and the Roman Catholic Church. The text opens with the statement on relations with the Roman Catholic Church, drafted by the Central Committee at Rochester in 1963. This statement declared that a genuine ecumenical dialogue has been established between the Roman Catholic Church and the other Churches, based solely on God's revelation in Jesus Christ and aimed at a deeper understanding, mutual enrichment, and the renewal of the life of the Churches, and allowing an approach to profound doctrinal differences in a spirit of love and humility. This statement urged all not to let any opportunity pass that might develop this dialogue on every level of the Church's life. A number of points were also indicated which demanded closer investigation so that a true dialogue could take place.

The W.C.C. prepares itself in various ways for this dialogue: it has sent observers to Vatican Council II, has discussed special matters (the laity, missions, social problems) with experts, and is in touch with the Roman Secretariat for Promoting Christian Unity. The Recommendation then states that the acceptance and promulgation of the decree has led to a "new situation": the Roman Catholic Church has expressed clearly and definitely her wish for, and her view of, the dialogue with the other Churches. In this the Roman Catholic Church has accepted the ecumenical principles and methods of the other Churches, at least in part; there remain important differences which must be clarified in open discussion.

The Recommendation then points out that a dialogue between the W.C.C. and the Roman Catholic Church is not a simple matter from the organizational point of view because of the peculiar character and limited competence of the W.C.C. This organization does not join in the dialogue which has developed between the individual members of the W.C.C. and the Roman Catholic Church, although the W.C.C. as such wishes to be kept informed and offers its services if requested.

The text then specifies the kind of questions that ought to be dealt with in the discussions between individual Churches and the Roman Catholic Church: (a) practical cooperation in matters of social service, social problems and international problems; (b) theological study programs to examine ecumenical relations (Faith and Order); (c) problems that are likely to create tensions between the Churches (*e.g.*, mixed marriages, freedom of religion, proselytism); (d) problems that concern the Church's life at large and that all Churches experience (*e.g.*, the laity, missions, etc.). Some questions will be dealt with more profitably on the international level, others on the national level. The Recommendation then makes the following concrete proposal:

"The foregoing considerations lead us to propose the setting up of a working committee, consisting of 8 representatives from the W.C.C. and 6 from the Roman Catholic Church. This committee should formulate principles and methods governing all future collaboration. When dealing with specific problems this committee should be able to co-opt qualified persons in an advisory capacity. The working committee would not be able to make any decisions but should work out proposals to be put to the bodies they represent and to be transmitted to the other member Churches of the W.C.C."

The contact already established between the W.C.C. and the Secretariat for Promoting Christian Unity would be maintained, as well as contact with the member Churches of the W.C.C. and the Churches who have not yet joined this body but have expressed the wish to do so.

Rome Accepts the World Council's Proposal

On February 18, 1965—the above mentioned "historic" date —Cardinal Bea, President of the Secretariat for Promoting Christian Unity, set out for Geneva to deliver Rome's reply to the Secretariat of the W.C.C. In his address of welcome to Cardinal Bea the retiring Secretary-General of the W.C.C., Dr. W. A. Visser 't Hooft, said: "It has struck me how often the words 'nevertheless' (*nihilominus*) and 'yet' (*attamen*) occur in the Decree on Ecumenism, This seems right to me. For true ecumenism is an attitude that is marked by these words. We do not underestimate our differences. We do not know how to overcome them. Ecumenism does not rest on the assumption that the differences are on the point of vanishing. It is based on the conviction that, in spite of the differences, we must talk together, and if possible work together. We take note of the fact that these differences exist and that they are as great as ever, but we add 'nevertheless', because our common faith in the same God, the same redeemer and the same Holy Spirit urges us to understand each other, to live together, as Christians ought to live together."

In his reply Cardinal Bea addressed those present (among whom the elderly first President of the W.C.C., Dr. Marc Boegner) as "beloved brethren in Christ". In these words, he said, he wished to sum up what we have in common through baptism, and our common root and foundation in love, and so "in Christ". After having offered thanks to God with joy for "this hour", he pointed to the long and laborious history that had led up to it. He voiced the joy of the Roman Catholic Church at the unanimous decision of the third Pan-Orthodox Congress (November, 1964) which urged its member Churches to continue and develop the dialogue with the Roman Catholic Church. He then proceeded:

"In the same way (as in the case of the Pan-Orthodox Congress) the Holy See greets with joy and fully accepts—and I am particularly glad to inform you of it on this occasion—the proposal made by the Central Committee of the World Council of Churches last month at Enugu to set up a mixed committee, consisting of 8 representatives of the World Council of Churches and 6 of the Catholic Church in order to explore the possibilities of dialogue and collaboration between the World Council of Churches and the Catholic Church. It is accepted that it is not the Committee's function to make decisions but to see on what principles and with what means such a dialogue and collaboration can become a reality. The results of the Committee's work will be submitted to the competent authorities on both sides for further investigation and possible decisions. I do not doubt that this measure, which corresponds so entirely to the letter and the spirit of the conciliar Decree on Ecumenism, will be most fruitful both for cooperation in the search for a solution to the great and urgent questions of our times, and for the dialogue in the strict sense of the word."

Cardinal Bea stressed that both he and his audience were fully aware of the "mountains of obstacles and difficulties" that all would encounter. "We have had examples of these in the events at the end of the third session of the Council and afterward. No doubt, more and greater difficulties will arise. The only thing that matters then is not to lose courage but to tackle the difficulties with fortitude and with that mountain-moving faith of which the Gospel speaks. No difficulties, of whatever kind, should be allowed to drive brothers apart in mutual mistrust. On the contrary, brotherly love and love of unity should inspire us to engage in frank discussion even of difficult questions."

Cardinal Bea concluded his address by referring to the hope expressed by Pope John when he summoned the Council, "that whatever the Holy Spirit brought about in and through the Council, may be a spur for our non-Catholic brethren to seek with still more zeal that unity for which Christ prayed and which he desired. If the realization of this unity is not only difficult but surpasses the strength and potentiality of man, we must put all our trust in Christ's prayer for the Church, in the Father's love toward us, and in the power of the Holy Spirit. 'And hope does not disappoint, because the charity of God is poured forth in our hearts by the Holy Spirit who has been given to us'" (Rom. 5,5).

The International Foundation of *Pro Mundi Vita*

The idea of *Pro Mundi Vita* was born of the conviction that the apostolic forces the Church has at her disposal must be distributed more scientifically over those sectors of the Church which are in need of spiritual help.

Better information, based on sound pastoral considerations and on serious socio-religious research, would help not only the religious orders and congregations, but also other institutions and organizations, clerical as well as lay, to devote themselves more efficiently to mutual aid in apostolic matters.

This vast project was set on foot by the Rev. Montanus Versteeg, O.F.M. His frequent discussions with bishops, priests, religious and lay people confirmed him in his conviction that it was most desirable to have objective information about the situation in those depressed regions, about the apostolic workers available, about the real needs and the means by which Catholic communities could be of greater mutual assistance. It is indeed understandable that every bishop or religious superior does all he can to reinforce the apostolic potential of his region or diocese. But it is also true that the various problems of local Churches demand a comprehensive approach, backed by numerous studies, projects and priorities, worked out in a scientific manner.

This is the only way in which effective assistance can be ren-

177

dered both in apostolic personnel and technical aids. A pastoral project presupposes first of all an objective assessment of the true situation. The continuous social changes caused by a rapid alteration of society demands that this study of the situation be continually brought up to date. At the same time constant contact between dioceses, religious orders, congregations and lay institutes (of which several exist already) is necessary in order to coordinate apostolic activity according to a comprehensive plan which is both supple and realistic.

These ideas were given shape in the foundation *Pro Mundi Vita*. The first conference (Maastricht, Netherlands, 1962) was limited to Brazil, and this was in order to provide Dutch religious congregations with information. Brazil was indicated as a first choice because the hierarchy of Northeastern Brazil had just started a concrete pastoral project, the elaboration of which was entrusted to a secretariat set up for the purpose. On the other hand, the *Conferencia dos Religiosos do Brasil* had organized a special orientation service for those religious institutes which wanted to start new foundations within the framework of that pastoral project. Thanks to the conference at Maastricht several congregations have started to work in Brazil with new foundations.

In September, 1963 Montanus Versteeg organized his first international congress in Essen (Germany) for a group of bishops, representatives of national religious federations (24 countries) and of lay organizations.[1] After this congress Fr. Versteeg established the definite structure of his work. Dr. Franz Hengsbach, bishop of Essen, and already President of the movement "Adveniat", accepted the patronage of the foundation. The Sacred Congregation of Religious, the Congregation of the Propaganda Fide and the Pontifical Commission for Latin America have sent delegates to the various congresses and continue to encourage the foundation. The General Assembly meets under the chairman-

[1] *La détresse dans l'Eglise et la tâche des religieux* (Depression in the Church and the task of religious orders). The proceedings have been published in German, French, English and Dutch.

ship of Dr. Dietmar Westemeyer, O.F.M., President of the Conference of Major Superiors in Germany, and comprises leaders of the Lenten missions in Western Europe, a number of national secretaries of Major Superiors' Conferences of various continents, representatives of some episcopal conferences, and the secretaries-general of CISG and UNIAPAC, international movements of Christian workers and employers respectively. Subsidies provided by the Lenten missions in Germany, Belgium and Switzerland, by *Oostpriesterhulp* (help to priests in the East) and by numerous religious congregations have made it possible to open a General Secretariat in Brussels.[2]

Fr. Versteeg's first aim is to create an international center for exchange and contact between the already existing documentation and information centers so that all those who are in charge will be better informed about the great needs of both the Church and the world, and about the ways and means of coping with them.[3] In order to achieve this, Fr. Versteeg has set up a network of permanent contacts with a great number of sociological and theological centers. At the moment he is trying to fill the remaining gaps in Europe and Asia.

After the second international congress which took place at Louvain in September, 1964 [4], he began to publish bulletins in five languages (English, French, Spanish, German and Dutch), addressed exclusively to the bishops, the major superiors, the leaders of the main movements of the lay apostolate and to spe-

[2] *Pro Mundi Vita*, 6 Rue de la Limite, Brussels 3, Belgium. The foundation, established by royal decree, is a non-profit-making society with international status.

[3] I quote Art. 2 of the constitution: *"Pro Mundi Vita* is an international society with a scientific and religious purpose. It serves the Catholic Church and its object is to gather, analyze and distribute in a scientific manner information about pastoral and social conditions in which the Church is concerned. This information deals mainly with: regional needs beyond the capacity of the local Church; the resources at the disposal of the Church, wherever they may be; the possibilities of forming a missionary force. The object of the society includes also any other purpose connected with it, such as the encouragement of research and the organization of scientific congresses."

[4] The main theme of this congress was the "universal responsibility of all Christians." The report of the congress has appeared under this title.

cialists in pastoral theology and missiology. At present about 1,000 bishops and more than 5,000 major superiors receive this publication.

The bulletins are composed according to French and English models (*Etudes et Notes Documentaires* and *Commonwealth Survey*) which aim at providing civil servants with information on actual problems and situations of which they must know the essentials in order to take correct and well-founded decisions.

In the meantime, Fr. Versteeg hopes that after the "running in" period the foundation will be sufficiently well established to deserve the confidence of leaders who could then ask directly for guidance on problems of the apostolate which it would be indiscreet or dangerous to convey by printed word. In the same way he admits that he is not as yet in a position to give immediate, intelligent and prudent advice on concrete and detailed typical questions, but he could help leaders to find the appropriate specialist, with the help of his already established contacts. More and more leaders have already appealed to him, particularly in connection with new foundations.

It is obviously not enough to be a good sociologist to ensure the orthodoxy of a "consultation center for apostolic productivity". A constant effort is made to maintain a dialogue with the best theologians and missiologists. This is the purpose of the regular discussions between specialists which are already taking place.

It should be noted that Fr. Versteeg neither can nor wants to be a substitute for the actual decision-taking. This is the responsibility of those in charge, whether individually or collectively, and there it must remain because they alone are the authoritative representatives of the Church and they alone know the limits and possibilities of the cooperating Christians for whom they are responsible. This, of course, in no way diminishes their duty to obtain the best possible information for their decisions. Fr. Versteeg aims merely at being an instrument among others to help them in this.

What the great industries, such as metal works, car factories

or even the hotel industry, can achieve in a short time with the
motive force of earthly happiness and man's creative will, Christians can achieve, too, if inspired by the needs of their brethren
regardless of race, creed or ideology, and moved by the Spirit.
They can do this even if it means hastening the process of the
Church's historical development and bringing about a somewhat
fundamental change in traditional pastoral methods. Here, Fr.
Versteeg's work may contribute toward a functional theology
which so many Christians demand today. I am thinking of a
theology that listens to God at work, not simply in the sacred
history of the past but in contemporary history, however disconcerting and exciting this may be. In this perspective, which
is that of the Council, Fr. Versteeg assists in that progress of the
spirit which shows in so many places. As such, his work follows
the Spirit of God in renewing the face of our old world.

BIOGRAPHICAL NOTES

JOHANNES METZ: Born August 5, 1928 in Welluck, Germany, he was ordained in 1954. He studied at the Universities of Innsbruck and Munich, earning his doctorate in philosophy in 1952 and his doctorate in theology in 1961. He is professor of fundamental theology at the University of Münster. One of his principal works is *Christliche Anthropozentrik,* which will soon be published in English translation. Among his other works is "A Believer's Look at the World," *The Christian and the World* (*Readings in Theology*) (New York: P. J. Kenedy & Sons, 1965). He edited a new edition of the two principal philosophical works of Karl Rahner: *Geist in Welt* and *Horer des Wortes.* He contributes regularly to theological reviews.

GÉRARD PHILIPS: Born April 29, 1899, he was ordained in 1922. He studied at the Gregorian University, Rome, earning his master's degree in theology in 1925. He became professor of dogmatic theology at the Grand Seminaire in Liège in 1927, and professor of dogmatic theology at the University of Louvain in 1942. He is the author of many theological works.

HANS URS VON BALTHASAR: Born in 1905 in Lucerne, Switzerland. He studied Germanic languages and philosophy in Zurich, and earned his doctorate for work on the "Eschatological Problem in German Literature". His many published works which have been translated into English include *St. Therèse of Lisieux* (Sheed & Ward, 1953), *Elizabeth of Dijon* (Pantheon, 1956), *Prayer* (Sheed & Word, 1961), *Theology of History* (Sheed & Ward), and *Martin Buber and Christianity* (Macmillan).

KARL RAHNER, S.J.: Born March 5, 1904 in Freiburg-im-Breisgau, Germany, he became a Jesuit in 1922. He studied philosophy at Pullach, Germany, taught at Feldkirch, Austria, studied theology at Valenburg, Netherlands and was ordained in 1932. In 1937 he became a lecturer in Innsbruck, Vienna and Pullach, and in 1948 professor of dogmatic theology at the Leopold-Franzens University in Innsbruck. After numerous theological writings (in which is expressed his central idea: an anthropocentric conception of the whole of theology), Rahner has come to be recognized as one of the most important theological thinkers of the German-speaking world. At present he is professor of Christian thought at the University of Munich.

HENRI BOUILLARD, S.J.: Born March 13, 1908, he studied at the Sorbonne, at the Jesuit College in Lyon-Fourvière and at the Gregorian University, Rome. He earned his doctorate in theology in 1941, and in letters in 1956. He is a lecturer in theology at the University of St. Joseph in Beirut, the Jesuit College in Lyon-Fourvière and at the Institut Catholique in Paris. His published works include *Conversion et Grâce chez St. Thomas d'Aquin* (1944), *Karl Barth* (3 Vols., 1957), *Blondel et la Christianisme* (1961) and *Logique de la Foi* (1964).

MAURICE NÉDONCELLE: Born October 30, 1905. He studied at the Sorbonne and at St. Sulpice, earning his doctorate in letters in 1943 and his doctorate in theology in 1945. He was professor of philosophy at the Ecole Albert de Mun from 1930 to 1945 and at the Catholic University of Lille from 1943 to 1945. He has been professor of fundamental theology at the University of Strasbourg since 1945, and dean of the Catholic Theological Faculty at Strasbourg since 1956. His published works include *Is There a Christian Philosophy?* (Hawthorn, 1960) and *God's Encounter with Man* (Sheed & Ward, 1964).

HEINZ ROBERT SCHLETTE: Born July 28, 1931, he studied at the Universities of Münster and Munich, earning a doctorate in theology in 1958 and a doctorate in philosophy in 1959. He also holds a degree in philosophy from the University of Saarbrücken (1964). Since 1962 he has been professor of philosophy at the Padagogische Hochschule in Bonn, Germany, and since 1964 a lecturer at the University of Saarbrücken. He has written a number of works in the field of theology, and is a regular contributor to numerous reviews.

JOSEPHUS FRANCISCUS LESCRAUWAET: Born June 19, 1923 in Amsterdam, Netherlands. He pursued his studies at the Catholic University of Nijmegen, Netherlands, and earned his doctorate in theology in 1957. He has published several works on ecumenism, and regularly contributes articles on ecumenical themes to *Oecumene* and *Tijdschrift voor Liturgie*.

International Publishers of CONCILIUM

ENGLISH EDITION
Paulist Press
Glen Rock, N. J., U.S.A.

Burns & Oates Ltd.
25 Ashley Place
London, S.W.1

DUTCH EDITION
Uitgeverij Paul Brand, N.V.
Hilversum, Netherlands

FRENCH EDITION
Maison Mame
Tours/Paris, France

GERMAN EDITION
Verlagsanstalt Benziger & Co., A.G.
Einsiedeln, Switzerland

Matthias Grunewald-Verlag
Mainz, W. Germany

SPANISH EDITION
Ediciones Guadarrama
Madrid, Spain

PORTUGUESE EDITION
Livraria Morais Editora, Ltda.
Lisbon, Portugal

ITALIAN EDITION
Editrice Queriniana
Brescia, Italy

DATE DUE

JA 19 '66			
FE 21 '66			
JE 7 '66			
JE 28 '67			
JY 26 '67			
FE 5 '68			
MA 26 70			
JE 22 83			
12-19-07			
GAYLORD			PRINTED IN U.S.A.